Who'd be a Mum!

'Mum, it's nice at our house,' Isobel said.

'That makes all the trouble worth it,' I thought to myself happily.

Then, unmoved she continued, 'But it's even nicer at Sarah's. They have apple juice there!'

For Hanna Ahrens, mother of four growing children, with her husband often away, there's never a dull moment. There are good days. And there are days when patience wears paper-thin, tiredness wins and tempers are lost. There are times of longing to be alone, of struggling to survive as a person, and as a couple.

Laughter and tears are often close in this warm and humorous account of family life – and a sharing of the things that help. There *is* someone who will always listen. Worries can be turned into prayers.

We pour out our love and our lives in this most demanding of roles, but we also receive it back many times over.

Love is the price we pay – and our reward.

For John, Suzanne, Michael and Isobel
because of whom this book nearly wasn't written
yet without whom it would never have been possible

WHO'D BE A MUM!

HANNA AHRENS

A LION PAPERBACK

Copyright © 1982 Brunnen Verlag, Giessen

Published by
Lion Publishing plc
Icknield Way, Tring, Herts, England
ISBN 0 85648 561 6
Albatross Books
PO Box 320, Sutherland, NSW 2232, Australia
ISBN 0 86760 470 0

First edition 1982 published in Germany
under the title *Schenk mir einen Regenbogen*
First UK edition 1983

Cover photograph: Lion Publishing/Jon Willcocks
Illustrations: D'reen Neeves

British Library Cataloguing in Publication Data

Ahrens, Hanna
  Who'd be a mum!
  1. Mothers
  I. Title   II. Schenk mir einen Regenbogen.
  English
  306.8'743   HQ759

  ISBN 0–85648–561–6

Printed and bound in Great Britain by
Collins, Glasgow

Contents

How this book began

As we were leaving the motorway and nearing home, Isobel, aged four, suddenly said, 'Mummy . . . can I have a rainbow?'

'A rainbow? I can't get you a rainbow!'

'Oh, go on! That one just now was so lovely – like a great big bridge. Do you think I could walk on it?'

'No, you couldn't.'

'What a shame.'

'Yes, isn't it.'

"Cos then I could walk up to heaven.'

'Would you like to?'

'Yes, just to see what it's like up there, and have one look at God, and then come down again.'

'Why?'

'Because . . . I don't know . . . when it's my birthday and you bake me a cake . . . I'm sure they haven't got an oven up there . . .'

Perhaps it would be nice to have a rainbow. Michael, my six-year-old, for whom nothing is impossible, then declared, 'I can make a rainbow!'

'How?'

'With our next-door neighbour's hose-pipe . . . you just have to hold it up to the sun and spray it.'

'Yes, but that isn't a real one'.

'No, but it's one I can make.'

Then in town one day, I came across some curtain

material with a rainbow pattern. I bought a metre and made Isobel a dress. And at play school a child said to his mother, 'Look Mum, there's the girl with the rainbow dress.' Isobel has her rainbow.

The dress is soon too small. But I hope Isobel will keep the rainbow in her mind for ever – a real rainbow, just like the one she wanted.

Children expect the impossible from their mothers. They have an endless stock of demands and questions. Unfortunately my strength is all too soon exhausted. I can only manage if I too keep asking, 'Can I have a rainbow?', so that I can know what God looks like; so that I can catch a glimpse of his love and goodness in the thousand little events of everyday life.

God has said, 'I have set my rainbow in the clouds, and it will be the sign of the covenant between me and the earth.' At the rainbow's end, heaven and earth seem to touch. In the midst of my daily life I should like to come back again and again to the place where heaven and earth touch, where God and I can talk to each other; where I can pray, 'Help me, Lord, to recognize you in everything I see. Meet me in the people I meet and the things that happen to me. I'm not asking for proof that you exist; but please let me see a little of your glory, and let me hear something in your Word to comfort me and give me strength. Make every day special. Talk to me often, because I forget so easily. Make me a rainbow!'

Hanna Ahrens

1
A day without love is wasted

Every chapter needs a beginning – especially the first chapter. But I can't think of one. I try asking my children. Michael says, 'Why do you write books anyway?' After this 'encouragement' I go round to my neighbours, but they are equally short of ideas.

My husband comes out of his room. 'You need a beginning?'

'Yes, an introduction . . .'

'Hm . . . I'm so shattered at the moment . . . can't think of anything off the top of my head . . .'

Then the front door bangs shut. 'Mum!'

'Yes?'

'Mum, I've got a new friend!' Isobel comes in singing.

'How nice! What's her name?'

'Dunno. But she's nice and she thinks I'm nice.'

'What did she say, then?'

'Dunno, she speaks French!'

Communication can happen even without words. But we need someone to say, 'I like you'. We need love and devotion, someone to listen to us. Michael's need for affection is almost greater than *one* mother can supply!

A day without love is wasted – for children and for us. But such days do happen. Days when I feel despondent and listless. The children are sullen, difficult, not as talented and lovable as I would like them to be. I reach the end of my tether and shout at them. Later, full of remorse, I try to apologize. 'I'm sorry I . . .'

But Michael interrupts me, 'It's OK, Mum, I'm like that sometimes as well. Mum, can I have a pair of football boots?'

We all need care and attention sometimes – but unlike Michael, I don't often say so. On the way back from the gym he sprained his ankle in the dark. Suzanne helped him home. He announced his arrival with loud wailing. We ran to the door to find him hobbling and moaning, while Susie explained what had happened. Theo provided ointment and an elastic bandage. The patient was let off all his household duties – no more tidying up or laying the table. All he could do was watch television and eat biscuits.

The next morning he couldn't dress himself. 'It's my foot,' he reminded us. I dressed him, and he was content. His sock wouldn't go over his foot, so he had to wear Isobel's slippers. Another victory!

After breakfast ('Do you want some more cocoa?' 'Yes,

please!') Michael says, 'Mum, I wish my foot was in plaster – then we could write on it!'

'What would you write?'

He gives me an embarrassed little smile. 'Poor old Mikey . . .'

'Yes, isn't it sad?'

A little while later, however, a little voice asks, 'Shall I take the bandage off?'

'No – why?'

'So that I can go roller-skating.'

'Doesn't it hurt any more?'

'No.'

The foot healed quicker than he wanted it to!

Things got rather worse when his sister became genuinely ill. I had just gone away. When I came back, a day and a half later, she still had a temperature. That evening we prayed that God would make her well. Then Michael chipped in, 'I'm not very well either!'

'Really?' I asked.

'Yes, I haven't had a bath for two days!'

'Was it so bad without me here?'

'Yes.'

Suddenly a loneliness I'd never suspected is revealed to me; an infinite fear of being deserted – but also a miraculous, extraordinary security . . .

Isobel is having one of her tantrums. 'I don't want to go and get my pyjamas!'

'No one's asking you to.' I am determined to stay cool!

'*You* go and get them!' she demands.

'No.'

In the midst of this, Michael puts his head in my lap and says, 'I'm glad you're still alive, Mummy. Will you die soon?'

'Are you afraid I might?'

'Yes. You see I'd like us to go to heaven together, so that I don't lose you up there!'

I explain to him that everything will be quite different in heaven, and that we can't lose each other there.

Yet when he comes home early from school one day and we've been delayed, he is sitting patiently on the doorstep. He beams as he sees us coming. Full of remorse, we say, 'Oh Michael, you've been here all on your own . . .'

'I wasn't on my own! I was talking to Tipsy!' Tipsy is our dachshund.

'But Tipsy's in the house!'

'Yes, we talked through the letter-box.'

'Oh good, then there were two of you.'

'Yes . . . well actually, there were three of us.'

'Three?'

'Yes, 'cos God's always here as well.'

I know that it's more important than almost anything to talk to your children. Actually, in our house it's the other way round. The children talk to me all day long. How I long for just half an hour in which no one speaks to me! Half an hour when no one says, 'Mum, my trousers are falling down! When are you going to put elastic in them?' or 'Mum, will you play with me?'

On the other hand, I could open the conversation myself sometimes! To get away from bits of elastic and playing snakes and ladders, I try asking, completely out of the blue, 'What do you think is important about our family?'

Suzanne, at ten the most sensitive and the 'peacemaker', says without hesitation, 'Getting on with each other. We don't mind if you get cross with us now and then, but we don't like you to moan at us all the time. And we like you to be here and play with us and be interested in what we're doing, and talk to us . . . but you do that anyway.'

'No,' says Michael, 'I think what's most important is for you to tidy up my wardrobe, else I can never find my toys.'

'Isn't it important for a mother not to be irritable, as well?' I ask.

'Why should you be irritable?' asks Michael. He's right. If our four children plus their three friends are roller skating in the house, I can always retreat into the bath! But then what do I do if just at that moment the phone rings?

We talk to each other a lot – at mealtimes, or riding in the car. In the middle of town, where the traffic is busiest (and I'm a bundle of nerves even without any children!) Isobel takes it into her head to ask, 'Mum, how do they make cheese?'

'I'll explain it later . . . oh, all right, it comes from milk. The milk gets left to go sour, then . . .'

'Yes, but how do they make milk?' My daughter is persistent.

'No one *makes* milk, cows have it in their udders.'

'But I mean how does the milk get into the cows?'

'Isobel, we'll talk about that at home.'

'Who stuck the cotton wool on the twig?' Isobel asked, when she saw the cotton twig that Yin-ling gave me yesterday.

In the middle of clearing away the breakfast things, I answered without looking up, 'That's cotton – it grew like that on the twig. There's a seed in the little ball of cotton, and the wind blows it about, like a dandelion clock, and where the seed falls a new plant grows.'

'But there's no wind or soil here.'

'No, we'd have to do it ourselves indoors.'

So we carefully picked the seeds out, filled a plastic egg box with soil and planted cotton. All chores were forgotten while we discovered all the things we could do with it. Matches became cotton buds and pipe-cleaners. We twisted the cotton into thread. Some of it was put aside to stuff a doll's cushion and some for cotton wool balls. Just a little was left on the twig in the vase, and Isobel ran to Miriam next door with the rest of the seeds, so that she could tell her, 'This is cotton. First you have to plant it, and then . . .'

Will the seed ever grow? At least Isobel now knows what towels and sheets are made of – and it was better than my explanation of how to make cheese!

'You're always having visitors!' Suzanne said to me one day.

Three times a week isn't 'always', but it is clearly too much for the children. They are jealous of the guests, who claim our undivided attention. Of course, children must learn that they can't always be the centre of attention, learn to be considerate and wait their turn, but . . .

So I ask them, 'Would *you* like to be my guests for once?'

'Oh yes! But you'll have to invite us properly, with a written invitation and all that!'

'All right.'

'In the post!'

'OK, and you'll have to accept or refuse – maybe on the phone.'

The 'guests' duly receive their invitations, with which they are delighted, and let me know from a local call box that they will be pleased to come. Yes, Friday evening will be fine. Seven o'clock then.

An hour before the great moment I go into the kitchen and ask if someone can help me prepare the salad and slice the bread – or have they become visitors already?

'No – visitors have to come from outside.' So we lay the table together. The chops are frying in the pan. For the sixth time Isobel asks, 'Can the visitors come now?'

'Yes, they can come.'

I wash my hands. If I'd had an apron on, I would of course have whisked it off now. The doorbell rings; the dog barks as usual. There on the doorstep are my four visitors: Suzanne in a long dress, clutching a bunch of flowers wrapped in paper; John looking very polite and almost making a little bow (he hasn't thought of flowers); Isobel jumping up and down with delight and Michael – well, Michael is dressed 'comfortably', in his old track-suit trousers and his polo-necked pullover with the holes in the elbows. But of course one doesn't mention anything like that to visitors.

'Flowers? Oh, how lovely! Daffodils – my favourites! They're the first I've had this year. Thank you very much, Miss Suzanne – that's very sweet of you.'

Isobel says, 'Mummy – I mean Mrs Ahrens – please don't think I haven't brought anything for you. I've made this house, with windows and a door that opens.'

'Oh, how gorgeous! Thank you very much. We'll put a little candle in it so it can shine through the windows. Would you like to sit down?' Michael is already at the table – without any hesitation he's chosen the most strategic place, next to the bowl of ice cream!

The food goes down well. Tea is the most requested drink, so that they can stay awake longer. Visitors can of course stay as long as they like – one can't send them home.

Isobel's tea is still too hot for her. She is sitting in her usual place beside me, so I feed her with a spoon; and because her rosy little face is glowing so prettily in the candlelight, I give her a little kiss. Suzanne is appalled. 'Mummy! You don't kiss visitors!'

'Oh, I beg your pardon!'

The telephone rings. When I say, 'Do you mind if I ring you back tomorrow? I've got four visitors,' my guests show undisguised pleasure.

Michael helps himself to sugar. A host is not allowed to object even to the second heaped spoonful. The proper thing to do is to look the other way. He has eaten plenty, but all the same I ask him, 'Would you like a little more meat?'

Michael, who has forgotten his part for a moment, replies, 'No, I couldn't, or I'll be sick!'

'Michael, guests don't say that sort of thing! You should say, "No, thank you, but it was delicious." '

'It was too. I've never had such good service. Is this a restaurant? I mean, could I order a Coke?'

'No. This is a private dinner. You drink what you're offered.'

'Oh, I see.'

'May I take your plates now? A little dessert?'

I clear the table. The children are a little embarrassed – but not enough to spoil their enjoyment of the whole affair. From force of habit, John reaches for the rice bowl, but I exclaim, 'Please don't bother'. He gets the point at once. It took a long time to teach them to help clear the table; on the way to the kitchen I wonder how long it will take to 'retrain' them!

Isobel spots a half-eaten piece of bread on one of the plates and runs after me. 'Mummy – I mean, Mrs Ahrens! Miss Suzanne hasn't eaten up her bread!'

Even when they are guests, my children don't seem able to stop telling tales! I suggest to my youngest visitor that she could give the bread to the dog, who seems to enjoy French bread with garlic butter.

While my guests transfer to armchairs and put on their favourite record, I put the dishes in the dishwasher. Meanwhile they settle down with cushions on the carpet. When I come back, Suzanne asks, 'Why do you like having visitors, anyway? It's such a lot of work for you.'

'That doesn't matter. I enjoy being with people I like – eating with them and talking to them.'

'And having flowers in the house as well?'

'Yes, that too.'

'Are visitors allowed to say what they would like to do?' John asks.

'If they and the host know each other well.'

'Well, we know each other well, don't we?'

'Indeed!'

'Then I'd like to watch TV.' And the others agree enthusiastically.

What can a hostess do in a situation like that?

The film turns out to be very boring, and so after a while the female guests wrap themselves up in blankets and sleep on the floor like sardines. The tea has clearly had a stronger effect on the men – John and Michael are quite awake and show no signs of going. Towards eleven I'm so tired that I'd love to go to bed. So I suggest that as they know their way around here, they won't mind if their hostess retires for a while. No, they don't mind – it's quite all right.

John helps me to lift Isobel, who is fast asleep, into the top bunk, where she goes on sleeping, fully dressed. Suzanne, half asleep, totters into her room, and I stagger into mine. Then Michael says, 'I'm coming too. You said you can't send guests away!' So he climbs into bed with me. 'Don't worry, I'm keeping my boots out of the bed!'

'Good! Sleep well!' I switch the light out and am just dozing off when Michael says, 'I think my bed's more comfortable after all, so I'm going. Thank you very much for having me. I'd like to invite you for dinner some time.'

'OK.'

'If I do, will you bring me something?'

'Yes.'

'Right, 'bye Mum!'

I fall asleep. Suddenly Isobel is wailing pitifully. Michael comes in to tell me that Izzy is crying – which I could hardly fail to have noticed. I send a message for her to come to me. She's had a nightmare.

'What did you dream?'

'I dreamt a thief came into the kitchen and ate all the sugar!'

'You'd better come and sleep here with me; Daddy isn't coming back till the day after tomorrow.' She falls asleep straight away, and so do I.

When I wake up in the morning, she is bending over me. 'I kept looking at you till you woke up. That was good, wasn't it?'

'Yes, it was. Good morning, darling!'

'And I've still got my clothes on from yesterday! Let's do that always, shall we?'

'Maybe not always, but it's nice now and then.'

'Are we still your guests?'

'No, now you're my children again.'

'Yes, we'd rather be your children, Mummy.'

'Why?'

'I just think it's better.'

At breakfast one morning Michael announces, 'When I'm up there, I'll ask if I can have a wish.'

'Up where?'

'In heaven, of course! When I meet God.'

'Oh, I see.'

'And then he's sure to say yes.'

I think to myself with a glow of pleasure, 'Well, at least he's learnt that much! He knows that God in his mercy will say yes.'

'What would you wish for?'

'If he says yes, I'll ask if I can have wishes for ever.'

'What for?'

'Well, suppose I want to wish that I can be clever without having to go to school . . .'

I hope God says no! But maybe in heaven the balance between what one would like and what one is prepared to give for it isn't a problem any more. And maybe then our wishes and prayers – if we still have any – will be the kind that God will indeed say yes to.

'You used to laugh more!' Suzanne declares quite baldly and goes into her room.

Her statement hurts me deeply. Even in the warm bath I shiver when I think of how irritable and unloving I've been with the children lately. I snapped at Isobel because she dropped her anorak and scarf on the floor like a snake shedding its skin, and her boots were left where they fell. 'I'm not a housemaid! Tidy your things up properly!'

She was so taken aback that she stood there unable to say a word. Then a little later, when she asked me if she could go to her friend's house, I said 'No'. It annoyed me that she would rather play there than in her own home.

Suzanne's things were lying all over the place. I asked her to sweep the room, but she did it so half-heartedly that I had to go over it again myself. I was furious; but instead of asking her to do it properly, I just shouted at her. And yet she's the one who helps me most often.

I'm cross because she doesn't know her multiplication tables yet. But isn't it my fault for not having enough patience and discipline to practise them with her every day? Then again, I'm sorry that I sent Michael away when he asked me to mend his wolf outfit. Only I was so tired just then . . . He'd been waiting for it for a week; but he saw that he could get nowhere with me at that moment, and said, 'Well, come to think of it, I'd really much rather be a clown. I can get things out of the dressing-up box in the cellar for that. Susie'll help me.' And soon a clown in full costume appeared before me.

I thought to myself, 'Maybe it's good if I don't always do everything for them – then they can learn to be creative and do things for themselves.' But John felt let down when I wouldn't help him with his homework on the Red Indians. I simply didn't feel up to refreshing my memory on the subject. He gave up the effort and left me with my guilty conscience.

Sometimes I just can't take any more. My patience wears paper-thin, especially if it's raining outside and I've got the children fourteen hours a day. On days like that I think to myself, 'How lovely a nine-to-five job would be! I could close the door and be alone. But I'm never alone. It starts even before breakfast: Mum? Mum!!!' I long so much to be alone, that I begin to feel guilty about it. I wanted four children, didn't I? I love them all, don't I?

It helps a bit when I can cycle to the supermarket in town to buy things for the weekend – toothpaste, salt, flour, margarine and milk.

When I think about this afternoon, I feel disgusted with myself. And yet I do love my children so much. Where would I be without them? My life is so bound up with theirs. I prayed so hard for these children, was so happy to have them; I've loved them, looked after them, worried when they were ill, stayed awake with them, got up for them in the night, carried them and comforted them . . .

'Lord, I don't understand myself! I don't like myself. Don't reject me! Give me new strength to meet their needs and answer their questions; more patience when they quarrel; the gift of reconciliation when they yell at each other. Give me tranquillity and cheerfulness.

'I am responsible for them, but they're your children. You made them as they are, with all their tiresomeness and lovableness. Help me not to spoil your handiwork; help me not to miss any chances. I talk about you so little – how are they to get to know you? What do I do all day, anyway? It seems such a lot – but what does it all add up to? I don't get round to doing what I really want to do. Do I even know any more *what* it is that I want? Some days roll over me like a huge wave. Evening seems to come so quickly, and then the next minute it's morning again. Lord, give me more love, understanding, warmth. Let them forgive me and not despair of me; don't let them give up and think it's not worth trying. Lord, it's hard to believe that you still love me.'

We all act as though we were going to live for ever. But what would I do, how would I behave towards my children, if I knew that I only had a short time to live? Lying in bed, I read another piece from Bonhoeffer's book of readings.

It's a comment on the sentence from the book of Revelation, 'Look – I am making all things new.' Only seven words, but to me seven words straight from God. There's nothing I need more than this. 'Look – I am making all things new.' As if deafened by joy, I fall asleep immediately, and sleep long and soundly. In the morning, all my burdens seem to have fallen off me. We have a lovely day together. I keep thinking: that is how God answers prayers. He hears 'the cries of the needy', as Psalm 34 tells us.

I will always thank the Lord;
I will never stop praising him.
I will praise him for what he has done;
may all who are oppressed listen and be glad!
Proclaim with me the Lord's greatness;
let us praise his name together!
I prayed to the Lord, and he answered me;
he freed me from all my fears.
The oppressed look to him and are glad;
they will never be disappointed.
The helpless call to him, and he answers;
he saves them from all their troubles.
His angel guards those who obey the Lord
and rescues them from danger.
Find out for yourself how good the Lord is.
Happy are those who find safety with him . . .
The Lord is near to those who are discouraged;
he saves those who have lost all hope.
The good man suffers many troubles,
but the Lord saves him from them all;
the Lord preserves him completely;
not one of his bones is broken . . .
The Lord will save his people;
those who go to him for protection will be spared.

With four children, the middle two need special care. Michael makes sure he gets it, but I have to keep an eye on Suzanne. In her case special care can mean getting up at 5.30 in the morning, waking her up quietly and sneaking out of the house to go to the park with a group of bird spotters, so that we can hear the birds and get to know their various songs.

Suzanne already knows about a lot of birds, and can tell you all about their everyday life and nesting habits – but getting up early to go and hear them in the park is another thing altogether.

'In the daytime you can only hear people,' she says, 'but early in the morning you hear just the birds and nothing else for once. It's lovely when it's so quiet. Afterwards school seems terribly noisy! Mind you, the hedge-sparrow is pretty loud – it sounds like a pram wheel that needs oiling!'

We've been going out with the group for several weeks. We know the birds' haunts – for instance, where the wrens live, the ones with the high trill in the middle of their song. We can spot the tree-creepers and the nuthatches who run up and down the trees like little mice but hardly ever sing. We can recognize the blackbird's excited staccato cry whenever a tawny owl or a squirrel approaches. The owl stares at us calmly from the fork of a beech branch. And all this on the edge of the city.

Then there's the swampy meadow with its cowslips and marsh marigolds, and across it comes the loud laughter of the woodpecker, that unprepossessing bird, followed by a regular tapping. We have learned quite a bit already; but 'It takes years', says our guide, Mrs Reger.

The main attraction for us is not the acquisition of knowledge – however interesting the calls and habits of birds may be – but our walk together in the fresh morning air. It's the way we stroll along side by side listening for individual voices, recognizing them or having to ask and then rejoicing in the thought that the robin redbreast is sitting on the path less than six feet away from us, putting its head on one side and looking at us. No one speaks. Watching and listening, observing and waiting – all this can only be done in the morning, before the day's business begins. The day will teach us other lessons – we will have to be quick-witted and shrewd, to talk and bargain, to stand our ground and fight for our rights.

Listening takes practice. The expert will be able to pick out particular voices from the general hubbub (now the white-throats and willow warblers have arrived . . .) I can only hear the clear, loud solos, the voices of the birds nearest to me. Mrs Reger says, 'Yes, I can tell these songs apart. I've been going out bird-watching for many years. I know birdsong pretty well. I wish I knew the Bible as well as that. Often it's a great incomprehensible jumble to me. But listening can be learned . . .'

Friday evening, just after eleven o'clock, I'm on my way home from Christine's birthday party. I'm on my bike, and because it's raining I'm going as fast as I can. At the last minute I spot a blue bike on a scrap heap. I know John is looking for old wheels as he's putting together a new bike for himself out of old spare parts. So when I get in I say to him, 'Get your anorak and wellies on quick!' (He's already in bed but still awake.) 'I've seen a blue bike with a saddle-bag and everything!'

The bike, however, turns out to be a moped and is unusable.

'Sorry, I couldn't see all that clearly in the dark.'

'Doesn't matter,' John reassures me, 'we'll find something usable in the end.'

Leaning on the back of a washing machine, there's a bike that looks like a film spool. Maybe we could use it to fix the wind-powered dynamo we're constructing on the roof . . . We're not quite sure yet how to make it, but Rolf will be sure to help John.

Unfortunately, the bike is totally rusted up. Then we find a table with quite new screws, bolts and tubular steel legs. And there are the wheels of that go-kart – surely we can do something with them as well . . . John has his tools with him. We take our time. There's no one left on the streets, and we're already wet through in any case. I don't know why I'm always a bit embarrassed about rummaging around in scrap heaps.

We get home soaked to the skin, change and have a cup of tea in the kitchen. We sit with our backs against the radiator and ponder how we can improve the design of the fan – not to mention how we can improve our lives. Suzanne and the little ones are asleep. Theo is away on an official trip to Papua New Guinea. We don't look at the clock, and I've no idea what time we eventually go to bed.

Maybe we'll be luckier next time. But happiness is not the sum of the spare parts you can find. It is the hour between twelve and one at night, when nothing's urgent or important except how to make a dynamo work so that you can get a light bulb to light up with it.

John, at thirteen the 'big one', with whom one can take so much for granted and leave so much unsaid, who goes to bed without help and looks after himself, sometimes needs someone who's interested in scrap. And I really am interested in scrap.

John is the one who helps to bring up the little ones, who takes responsibility even when he's not asked to, who uses my camera and mends my punctures. So I think he's grown up . . .

Then when he goes to try on a suit for his confirmation, he shakes his head, and instead of the suit we leave the shop with a sweat shirt and shorts, and everyone feels happier. For Christmas he asks for detective novels and a Bible with a zip, but the present we definitely mustn't forget is a big white toy dog at least three feet tall. As it's almost impossible to find such a thing and certainly impossible to pay for it, we buy instead some white fake fur and synthetic stuffing. We look for some eyes: soulful, black plastic eyes. I spend the next day at the sewing machine and that evening the dog looks at John with soft brown felt eyes. Plastic was too cold, somehow! There he lies on the bed, ready to give comfort when frustration and worry remain unspoken and problems can't be put into words.

'Christ will not ask us how much we have achieved, but how much love we have put into our actions.'

Mother Teresa

'I'd like to spend a whole day alone with you some time,' says Michael.

'Well, we could do that now and then!'

'No . . . I don't believe you.'

'Yes, honestly! What would you like us to do?'

'Oh . . . making something or baking biscuits . . . but just us two, no one else.'

'Or a bike ride?'

'Yes.'

'We could visit Auntie Cath.'

'Oh yes!'

We ring up and tell her that we're cycling round that afternoon for tea. She'll be glad to see us, she says.

Michael behaves so well that hints and meaningful glances are superfluous. He takes a serviette as instructed and eats his cake with a fork.

'More cream?'

'Yes please!'

He can hardly speak for delight.

And to make an afternoon of it, if not a whole day as requested, I suggest that we make a detour via the railway station. So we leave the bikes behind and go for a short train journey.

Michael hears a lot about saving energy, and if anything makes an impression on him, that does. He looks at the high vaulted roof of the station and decides it's a waste of building materials. Besides, it's all glass – bad insulation. And why all this neon advertising in the middle of the day? He'd have done it differently. He's against wasting money – but he has nothing against an ice cream . . . After a while all the noise gets too much for him. We travel back to the suburban station, pick up our bikes and ride home.

After this 'energy-saving outing' with cream cake and ice-cream, Michael is at peace with himself and with the world – and even with his mother. And the other three? I evade their glances and their questions.

When I'm putting Michael and Isobel to bed, I sometimes say, 'Dear God, thank you for our children . . .' That makes them really happy. They need to know that we're glad to have them. We ask God to keep us safe all night and help us to wake up happy in the morning. Amen.

Then Michael pipes up, 'What about the people who are ill or dying? You've left them out!'

'Yes, that's true. Let's ask God to be very near to them and comfort them.'

That comforts Michael as well, and he's ready to go to sleep. I give Isobel, who's in the top bunk, a kiss and sit on Michael's bed.

'Sleep well, don't talk any more!'

Michael wraps his arms around my neck like a sling. It's partly a sign of love, but mostly he just wants to hold on to me and delay having to go to sleep.

Isobel leans over from the top and calls, 'Go away, Mum! You cuddled Michael longer than me!'

'But Isobel! I can't start measuring with a stop-watch!'

'No, hang on! I'll get the egg-timer!'

Justice is half of life and envy is the other half. All right: three minutes by the egg-timer with each! After these six minutes of peace (when I want to say something, Michael protests, 'Don't talk! Talking spoils everything! I want to enjoy it!') we are tired out. I'd be happy to sink into the bunk and fall asleep. But then Suzanne appears. She gets the point of what's happening immediately and says, 'What a good idea – can I join in? Will you come into my room now?'

'All right.'

The egg-timer – which I originally bought to time the children cleaning their teeth (I've got a feel for how long eggs need to cook, which means in practice that the family get hard-boiled eggs, if any, for breakfast) – this egg-timer is now a measure of justice, an aid to giving love by the minute.

How differently, it seems to me, other mothers do things! They read stories until the children fall asleep. In our house it would be me who fell asleep! Or they bless their children. Michael's Godmother does this unforgettably. She makes the sign of the cross on her children's foreheads and says the blessing over them. How much it must mean to children, who like us have their worries and anxieties, stresses and sorrows, when they hear, 'The blessing of God the Father, who has made you so well; God the Son, who can take away all your sorrows, and God the Spirit who will bring you to heaven one day.'

'I've brought you a few flowers,' says Theo's secretary when she comes round for lunch.

'Oh, how nice! Flowers on an ordinary Thursday!' And I think to myself, Thursday 3 April, just an ordinary day. Or is it? Something about the date seems to ring a bell. Is it someone's birthday?

'Do have some more salad! A little more fruit juice?'

Now I've got it . . . 3 April! It's our wedding anniversary! And Theo forgot it! But then so did I. But it's *his* job to offer me a bunch of flowers accompanied by a kiss. I'm quite old-fashioned about these things. And instead of that he invites his secretary to lunch!

So, 'just in passing', I say to his secretary, 'The flowers are quite appropriate, actually – did you know it was our wedding anniversary?'

That was unfair. My poor husband! So I quickly add, 'Actually we both forgot about it.'

Later we make some plans: we'll celebrate late in the evening, when the children are in bed, just the two of us. We'll go for a Greek meal, and we won't talk about work or about the children; we won't mention the church or conferences . . .

We sit in the little 'Cretan' café. It's friendly, cramped, noisy and smoke-filled. No one can see anyone else for the fug, and no one can hear what anyone else says because of the noise. It makes it rather intimate.

We study the long menu. Seventeen years ago we went to Greece together.

'I'll have number four,' says Theo.

'And me. John needs new shoes . . .'

'Again?'

'Yes.'

'Sheep's milk cheese, twice, please. And a bottle of Retsina.'

'As a starter?'

'No, as a main course.'

We enjoy the evening – the music, and people around us whom we don't have to talk to. We don't talk much at all, in fact. Theo strokes the back of my hand. 'Would you marry me again?'

'You know the answer to that!'

'Yes, but tell me . . .'

'Of course I would! Pity I can only marry you once . . .'

We love each other and need each other a lot. Yet we don't often say 'I love you'. We should say it again, not just think it, even if we have been married sixteen years. And flowers on a Thursday – that would be nice. A luxury, but nice.

In October we celebrate our wedding anniversary again. In April, because we got married then, and in October, because we're still married. All around us, and sometimes in our own lives, we see that you can't take that for granted. So many marriages are like a fire that slowly goes out. In our experience, marriage is something too important to be left to look after itself. It's too precious to be grateful for it only once a year – to be grateful that God promised us his blessing when we got married, and that however much we neglect it or forget, that blessing can't be taken away.

So sometimes I cook a special meal in the middle of the week, just for us two. And sometimes, when I'm sitting at my desk, Theo comes and asks, 'Shall I get you something to eat? And a drink?'

'Yes, I'd love some.'

We need that kind of attention. Then it doesn't matter that Theo is away on trips for weeks on end. Marriage is not being chained to each other all the time; it's a blessing that one has to guard lovingly and carefully, but not anxiously. It's seeing things through the other's eyes; what does he need now? It's being able to say, 'I need you'. It's giving him a present, not because he needs it, but because I thought of him when I saw it.

God gave us marriage so that we could 'comfort and help each other'; so that we could encourage each other to face the day and its difficulties, the work we do separately or together; so that the other person can become what he wants to be, what he is meant to be – and most of all so that he can be happy.

'Jonathan went to David,' it says in the Old Testament, 'and helped him to find strength in God.' And I know that is what marriage is about, in the end – indeed, what all human relationships are about.

2
Dens, junk and happiness

'Only a childhood lived to the full will guarantee a life lived to the full,' says Dorothy Frutiger.

I agree wholeheartedly with her. And yet, trying once again to tidy up the children's room, I complain, 'Michael, what's that moss doing on the windowsill?'

'Don't you like moss, Mummy? Feel how soft it is – and isn't it a lovely shade of green?'

'Yes, I like moss too, but . . . oh, leave it. But what's a bird's nest doing on the bookshelf?'

'You don't understand – I want to keep it for the birds. Then they won't need to build a new one in the spring. I'll put it in the garden, and then I can watch them having baby birds and feeding them.'

'Well, that's a nice idea.'

Joy, enthusiasm, imagination – and knowing what moss

feels like – are more important than keeping things clean and tidy. The nest stays on the shelf.

Meanwhile I've discovered from an expert on mites that each nest harbours about a thousand fleas and mites, and that birds are right to build themselves new nests! But how can I explain to Michael what mites are? I only have the vaguest idea myself. They are so small, and Michael is so small, and he only wanted to help the birds . . .

Of course, occasionally, our house is spotlessly clean, tidy and quiet. It's like that at lunchtime on Saturdays, when the whole family has spent the morning cleaning. They all enjoy the result, but they also agree that it looks rather unnatural.

Sunday morning. Neither Theo nor I have to take a service today, so we needn't hurry. We're awake, but still in bed. There's such an unearthly silence in the house that I begin to get suspicious.

Michael is humming to himself. There's a sound of gentle splashing. Maybe he's having a bath? Why shouldn't he? The worst he can do is to let the bath overflow, and even that's never happened. He's too big to drown himself. No reason to get up. Yet after a while I call out, 'What are you lot up to in the bath?'

'We're giving some earthworms a bath – in the washbasin!'

As I'm well rested, I can suppress my disgust and the impulse to tell the children off, and answer in their own animal-loving spirit, 'Oh, the poor little worms! I'm sure they'd rather be dirty – that's why they live in the ground.'

'It's all right,' the reply comes, 'they're already dead.'

Here's my chance! 'Hadn't we better bury them, then?'

'Oh yes!' answers Isobel, 'in the garden! I'll go and look for stones and flowers for the grave.'

As this worms' funeral (in contrast to the funerals of dead birds) takes place without songs or tears, we can enjoy our

Sunday breakfast without too much delay. Meanwhile it starts to rain, and the garden becomes a sea of mud. Even the blackbirds decide it's too wet to hunt for worms. Uneasily I think to myself that any minute the children are going to ask, 'Mum, what can we do?' And I can't always think of something.

Then Suzanne asks, 'Hey, can we build dens on the landing, with chairs and tables and blankets and all that?'

'Yes, of course!'

They drag out old mattresses from the cellar, and other bits and pieces from their rooms. The house begins to look 'lived in' again – although you could also call it untidy. But the truth of it is, it's very pleasant. Little storerooms are set up in the dens, and stocked up with biscuits, nuts, sweets, whatever we've got. Oats, raisins and cornflakes will do just as well, as long as the basic need to provide against hunger and cold is satisfied. It's delightful to lie comfortably on a pile of old cushions and have 'something nice'. The little radio and the dog are invited to play too. It's a paradise of security, happiness and warmth which can be found nowhere else.

Their happiness is only increased when I crawl into the den too and read them something by the light of a table lamp. Dens are necessary now and then. But to put the parts of the den back in their places – that seems quite unnecessary to the children. To avoid that, they would rather rebuild the dens; make them into a circus, for instance. Cushions and mattresses become seats for the spectators, chairs are needed for the acts, blankets for costumes. Of course some additions have to be made: kangaroo furs, tyres, a clown suit . . .

The chaos grows as these changes are made. But the spectator has no time to think about that. He has to pay for his ticket and get a programme. Sometimes there are new 'numbers'; but Susie is always the lion, and Michael the ringmaster. Isobel takes on the duties of an usherette, and John, the 'grown-up' one, is the audience.

To swell the crowd, friends and neighbours are fetched. The kangaroo, also played by Suzanne, hops around and greets the audience with a handshake, showing them the baby kangaroo in her pouch. A big hand, please! In two shakes the kangaroo fur is turned round, the tail becomes a trunk and Susie is an elephant who can tap out numbers she 'reads' on a dice. More applause! After a brief interval the lion enters, with a grass skirt from New Guinea as his mane. He leaps through a ring of fire (the hoop is made of wire and has paper 'flames') and sits up and begs on a chair. Then the human acts follow: the clown who doesn't notice when his food is taken away, and the conjurer who writes in code or sometimes performs his eight world-famous tricks. Even when they don't work – particularly then – there must be applause, although the young spectators don't always oblige. If success won't come, Susie howls, 'I shall never, never do any tricks for you again! Never!'

'Don't be so upset, Susie, it happens to real conjurers as well.'

A door bangs – Susie has vanished into her room. The dog eats the last biscuit crumbs, and we try to make a passage through the mess for any Sunday visitors. The house is only really tidy when we go on holiday and take our mess with us.

We sit down in the living-room and go on planning our move into a terraced house. Everyone writes down what he wants in an old exercise book.

'You know what *I* want!' offers Michael. 'A jungle tree in the middle of the room, to climb up and sit in – and so that Izzie and I know where the line is between our halves of the room.'

'Michael, that's impossible,' we all chorus, 'your room isn't that big!'

'What a pity.'

'Besides,' declares John, 'you've already got your cherry tree. We'll take that with us.'

That cherry tree was a monument to Michael's persistence!

Michael's Godmother once gave him the book *The Golden Apple Tree*. It tells the story of some children who have a tree standing outside their window which bears golden apples all year round. Every morning they open the window and pick one.

'I wish I had a tree like that!' says Michael.

'Yes, it's a shame it's only a story, isn't it?'

'What do you mean, only a story? We could buy one – I mean a real apple tree. Or a cherry tree – I like cherries better.'

'We'll see.'

'Can we buy it tomorrow?'

'All right, we will,' says Theo.

We drive to a tree nursery and explain what we want.

'How much room is there against the wall of the house?'

'It isn't really a wall, it's a long French window. The tree would have to stand clear of the glass.'

'And how much room is there?'

'About eighteen inches, then there's a path.'

'Then you can only have a shrub-type tree; it'll grow about four feet high.'

'Right.'

A little trunk with three even smaller branches is dug up for us. In the catalogue it says these miniature trees bear fragrant giant fruit in enormous quantities, and it recommends supporting the bush with a stake. Fruit is promised only a year after planting, but what will we do till then?

Leaves appear, even three blossoms, but no fruit. Michael is confident: 'They'll come!' I can't share his faith. I go to the greengrocer's and buy cherries with their stalks joined in pairs, and hang them on the branches. To Michael they are 'his' cherries, the ones he was sure he'd get.

'Mummy? All my pets are ill and they need Elastoplast.'

Isobel knows that at the weekend I bought a six-foot roll of plaster, because a bike was being rebuilt and a windmill and nesting-boxes constructed in the cellar; because the children were going roller-skating and Susie was sewing a dress . . .

'Well, you can have a little.'

'I think,' muses Isobel, 'that I'll make a dot with a felt tip, to show where they're hurt, and you stick the plaster on. I'm the doctor and you're the nurse.'

'Fine.'

So we put dressings on all the favourite animals. It's a real international hospital: the pink glass snail from Venice, the zebra from Mexico, elephants from India, beetles trapped in resin from New Guinea, and from nearer home some plastic animals, Lego people and rag dolls. They lie side by side on a soft blanket and sleep out their convalescence. They're allowed to stay on my window seat over the hot pipes, since they're ill.

As far as I'm concerned the treatment is finished now – we've given them plenty of time and care . . . but Isobel says, 'Now we've got to sing.'

'Sing? What do you want to sing?'

'Christmas carols! If they think about Christmas they'll feel happy, and if they feel happy they'll get well, won't they?'

'Yes, I suppose so.'

'Silent Night . . . Good morning, children! But . . .'

'Yes?'

'They need something nice to eat as well . . .'

'What do they like best?'

Izzie says without hesitation, 'Fish fingers and tomato ketchup.'

As I haven't got any in the freezer at the moment, they have to be put on tomorrow's menu. Then I start looking at the pink glass snail towering over the abandoned zebras and wild boars, and think about the time when we bought it in Venice. We didn't buy it for its great beauty, but because Isobel knocked it off a glass shelf with her elbow and both its horns broke off. It was an expensive animal, too.

'Signora!'

'All right, I'll buy it!'

The fragile animal survived the rest of the camping tour with no further damage and we still have it today. Now at last its broken horns have been bandaged.

When Isobel acquired her snail, the others clamoured, 'And what about us? Don't we get any glass animals?'

Theo hesitated for a moment. 'Of course you can have some.'

Suzanne's glance fell on a delicate branch with two birds on it feeding their young in the nest. Even more fragile buds graced the ends of the twigs. How on earth would we get it home?

'No problem!' said the shopkeeper. 'We send those to America!'

'Sure – but not in a camping kit that has to be packed and unpacked all the time!'

We saw however that it would have broken Susie's heart to travel on without her birds. So the birds came with us.

'Thank you, Daddy!'

Crabs have eight thin legs. But the crab came with us too. Fortunately Michael only wanted two little birds, solid, tiny and not at all ugly. 'No problem!' we said.

Isobel went on looking round the shop. She found a plate with a colourful relief of a Christmas scene: chimney, Santa, tree, stocking, decorations – every detail of an old-fashioned Christmas, made in Hong Kong. Junk, but at least made of wood. And for Isobel, even in summer in the middle of Venice, there was nothing lovelier than Christmas. Now this festival – so long awaited and over so soon – could be with her all the time in a form she could see and touch. The joy of it kept her little soul tranquil for weeks.

There has to be some junk. How else could we appreciate the genuine article, or even distinguish it from the rest? Junk is fun, even when it breaks and has to be glued together.

'Only the children know what they are looking for,' said the little prince. 'They waste their time over a rag doll and it becomes very important to them; and if anybody takes it away from them, they cry . . .'

'They are lucky,' the switchman said.

'The Little Prince', Antoine de Saint-Exupéry

The line between freedom and recklessness is often a very fine one, and mothers balance on a tightrope between the

two every day. Of course, some toys are completely safe –
a magnifying glass, for instance. Not a cheap plastic one,
but a real one that magnifies properly – thirty times! That's
what we bought for Michael, who's so interested in flowers.
He'll learn a lot with that, we said to ourselves.

The present was a success. Michael magnified everything
– hair, skin, leaves, the bark of trees. Life was full of
interesting details. But the next day the sun was shining,
and the magnifying glass became a way of making fire. As
far as Michael was concerned, the present was now priceless
– you could create smoke and flames with it. This game
seemed a little too dangerous to us, especially when the
wind was blowing.

'Michael,' we said, 'the whole house could burn down!
Stop it, please.'

'OK.'

A couple of days later, Suzanne came into the house shouting, 'Mum, Michael's burning things again!'

Michael was lying on top of a wooden stagecoach in the
garden and wielding his magnifying glass. Something was
smouldering, and the rest of the world disappeared in the
haze.

'Michael, what are you doing?'

'Nothing! It's all right, Mum, I'm not doing anything
wrong . . .'

'Anyway, you're supposed to be doing your homework
– you've got to write "Tom" a hundred times!'

'That's what I'm doing!'

'It looks like it!'

'Look, Mum – you can only see smoke at first, but
underneath I've written "Tom". I just burned it in . . .'

And he had indeed – "Tom" was burned clearly and
legibly into the wood. Some things can only be learnt by
making a game out of them . . .

All the same, we wouldn't allow him to make a real fire. He knows that. As a substitute, and just for fun, I bought all the children floating candles. I gave them a big plastic bowl full of water, and some matches. They pulled the bowl into a dark corner under the bushes and were happy – at least, so it seemed.

I went round to my neighbour's to wish her a happy birthday. We were just having coffee when Mr Schipper, our other neighbour, came in. 'I just wanted to tell you that there's smoke coming from behind your rubbish heap . . .'

I dashed out calling, 'Michael!'

No reply. The smoke continued to rise. Mr Schipper, doing the only thing possible, directed his voice towards the rubbish heap.

'I'll get the police—they'll put the fellow in the nick.'

At that Isobel appeared, followed by Michael, whose eyes were streaming from the smoke. He trod out the fire, as he'd been taught, and emerged. As he was already severely frightened, a telling-off seemed superfluous.

Michael then suggested that he should go for a little bike ride to get some fresh air and then have a bath, 'so that Daddy won't smell the smoke.' Next I found him 'angling' in a puddle, with a worm dangling from a piece of string. I can't forbid everything!

How much more pleasant it is when he asks, 'Can I plant some weeds in a plant pot? I want to see if I can grow them.'

So we cultivate grass, herbs, dead nettles . . . The neighbours, too, prefer weeds to fire. They understand the desire to see something growing and not just to have the end product ready made. Together we build aviaries with nesting-boxes for the budgies and occasionally even weed the garden – why not?

Holiday-time at last! Yet no sooner are we in the car than I get that feeling that I've forgotten something!

'You always feel like that,' says my neighbour. But if only I knew what! It's the uncertainty that gets me . . .

A few miles south of Hamburg Michael asks, 'Mum – have you got my anorak?'

'Me? Why should I have it? Did you come out of the house with no jacket on?'

'Yes.'

So that's what I forgot! Now I can enjoy the journey. Another few miles, and Isobel asks for the first time, 'Are we there yet?'

To change the subject and because it's early in the morning, Theo suggests we should sing something.

'Would you rather have "Morning has broken" or "Rock of Ages"?'

'We don't know that,' chorus the children.

I only know it because it was our previous minister's favourite. So it's 'Morning has broken'. After the first verse we get a bit shaky on the words. I read out the second verse and then Theo says, 'That's enough, just read us the text for today.'

With a prayer for protection and for a successful holiday, our mobile morning devotions are complete, and we drive on southwards.

Yugoslavia is our goal; but since the rain is getting heavier and we want to keep our tents dry, we stop at a German youth hostel for the first night. So the tents stay tidily packed away, along with the cases, buckets and spades, beach balls, saucepans, airbeds, sleeping bags and blankets. There's a place for everything and everything's in its place. Without Theo's gift for planning we'd be all at sea. Even so, it seems a miracle to me that we can get everything back in after a night's camping. Later a water-container is added – at first a folding one which springs a leak straight away, then another folding one (to save space) with a closure which isn't watertight.

Then we acquire a twenty-litre canister, which we can't sell at the end of the holiday – either because of my French or because of some quality in the thing itself – and which has to come back home with us.

Soon we're on the way to Yugoslavia, and here on the other side of any possible Atlantic 'low', the sun is shining – though we don't see it at first, for it's already dark when we arrive. We take the first camp site that isn't fully booked and don't bother to inquire either about the price or how near it is to the Adriatic. We park, open the boot and take the tent-rolls out. They roll a little way, and the children make a grab for them. Setting up camp on a slope is an art we evidently haven't mastered. It's too dark to clear the stones away and to spot the thistles in time. If you're tired enough you don't notice either of them.

When we want to knock the tent-pegs into the rocky ground, the mallet, which Theo unpacked a moment ago, has disappeared. Even Isobel can't find it. Some Danish neighbours lend us theirs. We discover next morning that our own mallet is right under our tent – a safe hiding-place!

At last the tents are up. The children have started to blow up the airbeds. We hear them saying how dizzy it makes them. They sort out their sleeping-bags and track-suits, take a swig of squash from the two-litre bottle in the car, and evidently enjoy the whole thing thoroughly. It's their first camping trip.

We lie down in the tents with our feet pointing downhill. If you hang on to a tuft of grass, or whatever you can get hold of through the groundsheet, and at the same time push against the end wall of the tent with your feet, you can't slide downhill any more. Although—it must be admitted—you can't sleep either! At least I can't. Theo and the children are asleep. It's very cosy. The tent walls flutter in the wind like the sails of a boat. Only sails can weather a storm, and our tent can't! Towards morning, when the wind becomes a hurricane, the tent-poles collapse and the white 'sail' sags down on top of us. Luckily it's getting light, so we take the opportunity to get up. In the night Suzanne came out of the little tent, which promptly collapsed onto John, and joined us in ours, putting her mattress at right angles across the top of our two. All this achieved was to make us all slide down a little further. Experienced campers had abandoned the attempt to put their tents up from the start. They lay down under their awnings and weighted them down all round with stones – a safe, dry place to sleep even if from outside it looked like a cross between a heap of turnips and a burial mound.

Struggling against the wind and the slope, we try to roll our sleeping-bags up as tightly as possible and get all our things back into the boot. The children sleep on in the car. We pay our fees and leave this heap of thistles, stones and grasshoppers with its view over the Adriatic. The white breakers are amazingly beautiful in the first morning light.

We need new canvas and pegs for the tent and hot coffee for ourselves. Down in the harbour we ask the café proprietor, who speaks German, 'Is it always stormy like this here?'

'Storm? That's no storm. That's the bora! Look at the rocks over there: not a blade of grass will grow there – that's the bora! But you mustn't talk about the bora, or it won't go away.'

'I see. Does it come often?'

'Oh, not really. Only once or twice a month!'

So we've experienced something quite unusual. Not everyone's that lucky.

'How long does this . . . wind . . . last?'

'Afraid there's no knowing!'

Then it's better for us to leave it behind. We drive on south till the white crests on the waves get smaller. That takes us to the island of Pag, beyond Novalja. There's a camp site there. Are there any places free? 'There aren't any set places. If you can find a space you can stay.'

We find one right at the edge. Not under pine-trees, but a level, soft stretch of grass. We put up the tents in broad daylight. Even the mallet is there. The next campers are a satisfactory distance away. Now our holiday can begin. The sea is clear as glass. There is a narrow white pebbled beach.

'What, no sand?'

'No sand! Throw stones into the water!'

A gorgeous bay! So gorgeous, that more than 5,000 campers have come to it. To cater for them, two washing areas have been built and almost finished. If you can find them on the huge site, and if you can stand them, it's fine . . .

The camp warden is uncommunicative about these arrangements. 'Temporary water shortage,' he says. He's right, too.

It's holiday time everywhere, and every time we come back to our tent a new family has moved in near us. It's amazing what tiny gaps people take for free camping spaces. Neighbours who come too near get a stony stare for a quarter of a minute – if they can withstand that they can stay. Most do. There are only two families from our home-town, with children and transistor radios, whom we can persuade to move elsewhere. Actually it wasn't where they came from that bothered us, only that they argued in non-stop dialect about who had made the hole in the airbed. We are supposed to be on holiday in Yugoslavia, after all!

Someone informs us that at 5.00 in the morning there's a good chance of getting a shower. But as we don't have an alarm with us there isn't much chance for us. We prefer to swim straight across the bay first thing in the morning and then run back across the still cold stones of the beach. After that a hot coffee is gorgeous. I enjoy it particularly because Theo makes it – strong, Turkish coffee with sugar.

In the course of time our behaviour to our neighbours changes drastically. Since they're there in any case, we give them sun-tan oil, drinking water for their coffee and left-over tomato soup. Even those who come too near for comfort get a friendly welcome: 'Of course there's still room!' Theo – barefoot – helps them to push their trailer onto the thistle field, while I make them some squash. Clearly we have got used to having people around and given up our dream of a deserted Adriatic beach.

The children are uncomplicated and get used to every situation. Occasional temperatures and diarrhoea are treated with tea and dry biscuits. Since we cook as little as possible, they are always hungry and eat everything. No one complains about the fact that there isn't much apart from spaghetti, soup, white bread, pancakes and peaches. We buy wine and ice cream and even manage to procure a kind of peanut butter. So the problem of nutrition is solved. Only twice do I come to the point of giving up cooking altogether – but that comes later, in France.

We travelled through Provence into the Camargue. Free camping right by the sea, but the nearest drinking water is eleven kilometres away. Ten thousand campers, flamingos and salt water lakes, fish swimming in the big waves, shown up clearly by the bright sky. Sunsets – and stormy weather again. No, not a storm – this time it's the mistral, as our neighbours from Marseilles inform us. This is supposed to be a good thing. Without the mistral the mosquitoes here are unbearable. So we've been lucky with the wind again.

But in spite of digging a ditch in the sand we can never succeed in getting the water to boil in our little calor gas cooker. An attempt to make pancakes, sheltered from the wind in a saucepan, also fails. Another time, in Provence, Michael wants cold tea. He's got diarrhoea, caused by ice cream, peaches and long swimming in cold rivers.

I put on some water, in a pan with a lid. Just as it's nearly boiling, Suzanne trips over my careful construction, which I've left to itself in a sheltered spot by the tent wall. She escapes without scalding herself. New water is fetched and a second attempt made. Half-way through, the hissing of the cooker suddenly stops – the canister is empty. Such things will happen. John screws a new canister in. Eventually – it takes long enough for me to do the washing and get in a little sunbathing – the water boils. I make the tea and let it cool. When it's ready, I shout, 'Michael – your tea!'

Michael answers, 'I don't want any tea!'

Well, apart from the cooking we do very well. Especially where the weather's concerned. We've only had one night of rain, and that was in Yugoslavia. Our tent is supposed to be rainproofed, but it rains through in spite of that. Spray falls on our faces as if out of infinitely fine watercans. Refreshing at first, it soon becomes a nuisance. In the grey of morning we creep out of our tents and hoping for sympathy, tell our neighbours, 'It's raining through on us!'

'Just a drop of rain?' say the others, 'our mattresses are floating!' It'll all dry out again!' But we crawl around on our knees mopping while the others do nothing at all. They sit in front of their tent in the morning sun and drink coffee, just as people are supposed to on holiday.

Our Dutch friends leave. Before they go we make them more coffee with milk and sugar and give them a hearty farewell. We are becoming more popular by the minute. Earlier they implored us to go to central Yugoslavia, to see the national park and the waterfalls. They described the way to us so elaborately, with maps, postcards and bits of advice, that it seemed almost a sin to go straight on to Italy. We promised to leave nothing out. It's time to leave in any case – two new tents have spoilt our view of the Adriatic, and there are lines of washing hanging everywhere. There is a long queue for drinking water and next door someone is frying the fish he caught last night. There's a young couple who keep saying, 'Marriage is rot!' Their tent is so small that the dog can't get in. We are beginning to feel as if we were in a refugee camp. So we pack our things, which in the end is easier than tidying up. Then we drive back the way we came – from the island to the mainland, then along the Adriatic coast. Strenuous, but beautiful. We spot a little church with a tower on an outcrop of rock. I'd like to stop and sit there for an hour, without talking, without doing anything. It looks like a place where heaven and earth meet. I long for quiet and meditation – but we've already passed it and are driving over the steep coastal mountains on the way to the national park and Postoina.

The park, which we had imagined as a kind of primeval forest, turns out to be a thoroughly commercialized enclosure with cobbled paths and a regular pattern of trout ponds (fishing with permit only!) and souvenir shops. Crowds of people surge along the numbered paths. The scenery would no doubt be lovely if one could only see it. But that's impossible – to try would inevitably mean treading on the heels of the person in front.

The caves in Postoina, with their famous ancient fish and their underground river, are indeed spectacularly impressive, but very cold. All the sights have to be seen in groups. We've not yet succeeded in getting away from the general stream of tourists. If that's still possible at all in Europe, it needs many more original ideas than we have. Someone tells us it's still possible in Finland. But that's too far for us.

Our provisions are gradually running out. We haven't had shampoo for a long time – washing up liquid will do just as well (indeed, it gives a much-prized extra shine!). I clean my leather sandals with a real sponge from the Adriatic, dipped in sun-tan oil. In spite of these drawbacks we travel on to Italy. It seems to happen of its own accord if you follow the road.

We come into the area around Venice, to Punta Sabbioni. Another wild camp site between pastures and sand-dunes. We prefer this to the overcrowded official sites, which are also very expensive, since they offer yoga, discos, a Catholic mass and ten-pin bowling. The children can put up their own tent while the exhausted adults go on a hunt for drinking water.

From a nearby derelict bunker we fetch a couple of blocks of concrete which will serve as a table and chairs. Thus we escape the half-crawling, half-kneeling position which gets rather demoralizing after a while. Upright and free, we sit and fry ready-made hamburgers. There's spaghetti as usual, plus wine and milk. We are completely happy. Venice, sensed rather than seen through the mist, lies before us across the sea. Tomorrow or the day after – no one can tell us what to do – we'll go over there by boat, so that the children don't miss this glimpse of art and culture, history and wealth. We want to see everything – the Doge's palace, the art galleries, the cathedral and St Mark's Square – as long as we can stand up in the heat.

To save money and because of the heat, we've taken bottles of orange juice and peaches with us. To stop the peaches getting any more mushy than they already are, we eat them first thing in the morning in a corner of St Mark's Square – and the pigeons don't get any.

At this point we don't yet know that we won't find a tap

to wash our hands until the evening. In fact the whole of Venice seems only to have two toilets. The number of such facilities seems to bear a remarkable inverse ratio to the number of 'sights'. We take this as a sign that for such purposes one has to find a restaurant.

On account of the size of our family and the staggering level of the prices, we pick out a snack bar. Six portions of spaghetti – £5.00. The service and clearing up are so quick that the children don't have a chance to finish their cokes; and our other 'plans' can't be carried out there either.

Everywhere there are groups, couriers, commentaries in all languages. A woman is holding a faintly whirring portable fan in front of her face. There must be a way to experience Venice and survive! 'A day like this isn't much of a rest . . .' I hear a father say. He has said what I've been thinking. I turn to him gratefully.

The works of art are lovely. Churches, uplifting and at the same time appalling in their splendour – but with sticky hands? Venice should be visited without children, without peaches and without orange juice. Maybe in winter, when you can see a bit of the marble floor of the cathedral.

In fact there are many things we'll do differently next time. We ought to take fewer clothes, more camping equipment and a tent frame that stands up straight on any incline. We need a little table and two chairs, so that we don't have to endure seeing how comfortably others lie in their camping chairs, coffee and radio before them on the table, while we kneel in front of our cooker and wait to see if the water is boiling yet or not. A cooker that cooked would be nice. We'd be better able to weather the storm – I mean the very useful mistral – in the Camargue if we could wash the sand from between our teeth with hot tea.

And we want to go to Provence again, to our river and the pine tree in whose branches Michael hid a particularly

DENS, JUNK AND HAPPINESS / 51

nice stone. We'll find it again, it was on the left before the bend in the road . . .

After five weeks, when we arrive back in our house in Hamburg, it seems like a huge grey palace with loads of right-angled rooms. There are five taps and real toilets, but no flamingos or salt lakes, no queues or fishes, no rivers or rocks, no sea and no pebbles.

We're already looking forward to our next holidays with the bora and the mistral.

3
Who am I?

I know children need a mother with strong nerves. But now and then mothers need friends and neighbours with strong nerves too, friends who will say, 'The children? No problem – send them to us! Yes, the dog as well, and go away somewhere with your husband.'

So off I go with Theo to a theological conference in London, as a guest. And someone greets me with the words, 'And who are you?'

'I'm Theo's wife.'

'Is that all?'

'I think it's quite a lot!'

The answer is a friendly smile. A little later someone else asks, 'And what do you do?' I've learnt from my first experience; this time I say, 'I'm a minister.'

'Oh, how interesting!'

Being a wife and mother has no status as a career. It's described in negatives: 'only a housewife'. The housewife's work has no lasting end products; it goes unnoticed and unrecognized – because it's unpaid. It's a job with no fixed hours, no holidays, no training schemes and no pension.

No one sees what a mother does – except when it's not done. Only then does anyone notice the general untidiness, the piles of dishes and washing, the trousers full of holes; the children who arrive at school late, with no packed lunch, and who don't know the answers to their homework questions. But of course that doesn't happen; for mother is always there. Indeed, it's being there all the time that wears her out. It's a real problem.

But I could look at this impossible career in a different light. I don't have to dwell on the lack of public recognition and official wages – I could look at things more cheerfully. Instead of fighting angrily for my 'rights', protesting against the whole world and especially my husband, I could be thankful for the love and happiness I experience through him. Without his love the whole thing would be meaningless. I could enjoy the luxury of being my own boss and deciding for myself what's important and what isn't. I could be glad that I have time for the people around me.

I can, for instance, have coffee with my neighbour in the middle of the morning. Or I can sit down at my desk and write a letter – not because I have to write it, but because I feel like writing to someone who will listen and understand. Of course I'll be disturbed by interruptions. 'I wanted to come and sit with you,' says Isobel, 'so that you wouldn't have to sit on your own.' How nice not to have to live alone!

Being alone is harder to bear than having children who grab hold of my knees with sticky fingers and say, 'Try this soup – I made it myself. The red colour's because of the ketchup.'

Thankfulness and joy are a good antidote to frustration. I don't often realize how well off I am. I don't appreciate God's rich blessings; I'm blind to his protection and his mercy. But the God who makes the blind see can open my eyes, too: he can make me observant and sensitive. He can change the way I do things and the way I deal with people; he can help me to understand what the Bible says and to act upon what I read. For, as the apostle Paul says in his letter to the Colossians, God has chosen us to be his people and has given us a new kind of life. His deep love and concern for us should encourage us to treat others kindly – not bearing grudges, but being gentle and ready to forgive.

'Have a nice evening!' my sister-in-law said to me on the phone.

She'd rung after eight because she knew the children were in bed by then. I didn't disillusion her. And it is true that later in the evening I did actually manage to do some reading. What I read was that a mother who looks after her own happiness will be able to help her children lead a happy life. Happy mothers mean happy children – who could deny that? I'm all for it!

Happiness, for me, means just occasionally being able to sit alone with a book and keep the thread. Or being able to listen to a record without someone interrupting to ask, 'And when can I listen to *my* record?' or singing something quite different in competition to it. Happiness is being able to write a letter without rushing it, or being able to do just one thing at a time.

My happiness, in this case, lasts about seven minutes.

Then Suzanne comes out of her room. It's about half past nine. She's wide awake and highly excited.

'Mum, my hyacinth's got a new shoot! Will it become a flower? It looks so funny . . . it's on the side nearest the light . . .'

So I have to go and have a look. There's a new bulb forming – no, two! I've never seen anything like it myself. 'It's making sure it has flowers next year, isn't that great?'

'Yes . . . sleep well, Mummy.'

'And you.'

'Mum . . . will the hibiscus be all right if I open the window a bit?'

'No, I don't think so. It's freezing outside and the plant's just growing new leaves. Open the landing window instead.'

'OK, sleep well!'

'And you.'

'Mum, the landing window's stuck 'cos we never open it. Can you get it open?'

'All right.'

The flowers have their warmth and the children their fresh air; so I sit down at the desk again. Now the dog wants to go out. No problem – I let him out into the garden as usual. But it's too cold for him and he wants to come in again straight away. Someone sets off a left-over firework. The dog, easily frightened, starts to bark. He won't settle down again. Michael wakes up and starts to cough badly.

'Mum, can I have some cough syrup?'

'OK.'

'No, I want the one out of the brown bottle, the one that tastes like boiled sweets, do you know the one I mean? In the adverts on telly today . . .'

'Yes dear, now go to sleep!'

'And you!'

Now the dog's scratching at the other door. Before the claw marks get any deeper, I quickly open it. He's remembered that he'd left a bone outside. He brings it into the house and crunches it up on the carpet. When he's finished I sweep the bits to one side and put the hall light out for the sixth time. The dog lies down to sleep. If Isobel doesn't get a nose bleed now and if none of the budgies is ill, I've got a quiet evening in front of me! At eleven there's a Japanese feature film I want to see, 'A woman should be like a rose'. Michael seems to need poetry at this time of night too; I can hear his musical clock playing, 'Ladybird, ladybird, fly away home . . .'

The film is boring; maybe I'm just too tired. I should have gone to bed. But I'm not just a cook, night nurse, cleaner, dressmaker, waitress and entertainer for my children. I like work – I work fast and I work hard – but I can't live by work alone. I need time off, time to myself, to read and listen, to reflect and pray – even if it's late. Otherwise my day slips through my fingers and I end up discontented and unfit for human company.

I need a change from all the tidying up, running to and fro, getting up every few minutes. If I want to make the bed in our bedroom and I pass the children's rooms on the way, I never get to our room. All this constant interruption is tiring; if I don't rest I'm soon exhausted. But the strength I get from prayer keeps me going.

'Do you have to start building a plywood boat three days before your confirmation?' I ask John.

In reply he asks whether I'd rather he went out and smoked in the street with the others.

'No – I was just thinking about the woodshavings and stains and all that . . .'

'But you're usually so keen for us to make things ourselves.'

'Yes.'

And I am really keen for them to play and develop their imagination. But who clears up the bits after the cutting, glueing, painting and sewing? Pets are important, too; but who looks after them when the children forget? Baking biscuits is fun, but who scrapes the dough off the kitchen floor? And who keeps on buying new ingredients? The shopping is a particular nightmare for me.

In the middle of this nightmare, the doorbell rings. 'I was just passing by,' says Betty, 'and I thought I'd see if you were in.'

'How lovely! Do come in. Actually, I'm always at home. I was just thinking that in the last three years I've carried 2,000 litres of milk – from the shop to the car, from the car to the house, and the empty cartons out to the dustbin. And that's just the milk! It's incredible how much food gets sluiced through our stomachs. And then there's the cooking, and helping the children with their homework, which usually means tantrums . . . I feel like a chair that everyone collapses into!'

'Come on,' says Betty, 'let's have some coffee to start with. It's so warm we could almost sit outside . . .'

'Do you take milk?'

'Yes, please.'

'I'm sorry, I didn't want to dump everything on you like that. After all, with your five you've got more to do than I have.'

'No, I don't think so. Our children are older than yours – and they've learnt that I can't be there all the time. This afternoon, for instance, I just went out. I refuse to be an armchair for everyone. I don't think that's right. After all, I get tired sometimes, and I have my own needs and plans. They have to take that into account. You know, if I deny myself everything now, then later, when the children leave home, I'll be quite drained and empty. I won't have any strength left for my own life.'

'And do you manage to get it into their heads that you have needs of your own?'

'Most of the time. Of course the family has priority, but I'm not prepared to be available all the time. I need some space now and then, and I enjoy them all the more for it.'

'Yes, I'm sure you're right. But while the children are small there's so much to organize before you can go out, that most of the time it's just not worth it. And actually I quite like being at home. I have everything I need around me: my table, my scissors, paper, paint, typewriter, sewing-machine, recorder, books . . . and I don't carry cartons of milk *every* day . . . You know this coffee is doing me good, and so are you.'

'All the same,' says Betty as she gets back into the car, 'do go out some time. Leave everything behind you for once.'

A week later, when I've bought my rail ticket, I go to the kiosk and buy four little souvenirs for the children. And I tell the elderly lady sitting opposite me in the train all about my lovable, original family – even though she hasn't asked me about them. I can't help being a mother!

Occasionally I think how nice it would be to have time to myself – without the constant bickering of the children.

'Mum, Susie keeps annoying me!' Michael comes running into the large living-room of our holiday home in Denmark.

'Michael annoys me too!' Susie complains.

'Yes, but not for so long!'

'Do you know something,' I chip in, 'I'd like to be alone for once. I want to take a walk along the beach.'

Silence.

Michael is the first to recover. 'Oh, yes, I'll come with you!'

'But I wanted to go on my own, that's the whole point . . .'

'Yes, just us two, all alone!'

'Oh very well, just us two.'

'And what about us?' cry the others.

'We'll go too, and then we'll meet you quite by accident,' suggests Theo.

'No!'

In the end I really do go out on my own, to a wool-dying factory, because I'm interested in dying textiles with leaves and yellow-wood. In Papua New Guinea I used to dye wool myself, with tropical plants and tree bark.

The family goes into the village to buy ice cream, and they survive an hour without any noticeable harm. So that evening I summon up the courage to say, 'Do you know what? I'd like to have a day off once a month.'

And since we're on holiday and everyday life seems a long way off, everyone says, 'Of course you can! No problem!'

Theo is very much in favour of it, too. It gives me a great feeling of freedom and relaxation. It makes no difference that we both sometimes forget about the day off, and that especially in months when we've travelling it has to be left out. In principle at least, I have my day off.

Thank you, Lord, that I have a family. My life has a purpose, because I can be there for them. But sometimes I'm tired and resentful, for often they don't notice how much work I do for them, and how my own needs and

wishes get left out. Help me to distinguish between necessary sacrifices and unnecessary self-denial caused by
burdens I've taken on myself. Give me courage to create
my own space, the space I need for my personal growth.

Women's day of prayer, March 1980

John comes into the kitchen half asleep, collapses on to the
yellow metal stool and says, 'Seven hours and then Mrs
Kampe in the last one, great! It really finishes you off.'

'Yes, I think seven hours is impossible too. It's only
because you have Saturday off. Five hours a day would be
better.'

'But school on Saturday would be the end. There'd be
no time left at all to recover!'

Susie comes in. 'Why did you wake us up so late?'

'It's just that you took so long to get dressed! Has the
dog been fed yet?'

'No, you didn't give me any food.'

'You should look after your dog yourself.'

She fetches a filthy dog bowl.

'Susie, you'll have to wash that first!'

She tries to, but the food is firmly stuck on.

While I'm scrubbing it with an old scouring pad, I say,
'You want to do all kinds of things – be a vet, make films
about animals, do animal research – but looking after one
dachshund properly is too much for you. Animals mean
work, you know . . .'

Meanwhile Isobel staggers into the kitchen. 'Mum, I
want to eat too!'

'Izzie, go back to bed till the big ones have gone out.'

'No.'

'Then sit down here on the stool.'

'No, I want to sit on the radiator like John.'

'All right, I'm going!' says John; and Suzanne goes ten minutes later.

Michael arrives, in a bad mood as he always is first thing in the morning. 'Why are you so rotten to me? You opened our window and the wind blew my poster off the wall. Now there's a crease in it.'

He's furious. I go and hang the poster up again and say, 'I only wanted you to have some fresh air while you were asleep.'

Michael notices the empty dining-room table and says, 'Why isn't breakfast ready?'

'It is ready, it's on the kitchen table!'

'I don't like crispbread! You know I don't!'

'Then have some white bread. We've got to bake some brown. You two can help me with it, then you can have the measuring spoon and the flour bag to play with.'

We bake the bread, and the world becomes a calmer place. Both children now want to play out in the sandpit with spoons, bags and bowls. The sand is still covered in hoar-frost, but they dig deeper, and play as if it were summer. However, they can't stand it for long; just long enough for me to have a second cup of coffee and read the Bible verse for the day, and the extract from the letter to the Hebrews on which I have to preach in two weeks' time.

The front door opens. Thinking it's the children, I call out, 'Well?'

A voice answers, 'Hello?' But it doesn't sound like Isobel or Michael. I go to see. An old lady in a grey coat and a red hat is standing in the hall. 'Is this where the English lessons are?' she asks.

'No, it's next door.'

'So sorry!'

'It's quite all right.'

The bread has to go in the oven now; the dog has to go out, the dishes into the dishwasher, and the washing into the washing machine. There's a letter to post, the children's bedrooms and our room to clean . . . I'm already looking forward to the afternoon when I can work on my sermon in peace. At half past two John comes home.

'That school is an absolute pain in the neck, it's so dreary and boring . . .'

I can't stand all this complaining any longer. 'Do you know, you may well be right!' I answer. 'I'll come with you some time. I'd like to see what it's like to sit in a classroom for seven hours.'

'You wouldn't, would you?'

'Yes! I'll write to your headmaster and ask him to let me.'

The headmaster does let me, and the teachers agree. The other pupils think it's a brilliant idea. I sit in the back row.

The teacher comes into the room but no one takes any notice. He sits on his desk and waits for the hubbub to die down. He's hoping that his silence will influence the class. But they're more thick-skinned than that. And the scraping of chairs in the class above adds to the racket. As soon as the class is relatively quiet, the teacher takes the opportunity to begin. After twenty minutes it's impossible to concentrate on his subject any longer. He gets the class to write. One pupil unpacks his lunch.

'Can't you eat at break-time?'

'Yes, but it's more fun in lessons!'

How long an hour is! I'd forgotten. And we have to get through seven of them!

In the second lesson there's a woman teacher. She explains things clearly and well, but does nothing about the fact that everyone is talking at once. She gives the impression of being tired and without any enthusiasm. Next there's a supply teacher who's supposed to be teaching maths; we've been joined by another class. The pupils show no interest.

'We'll do your sums as soon as you've done the one we're going to set you,' they tell her.

There's a damp board duster stuck on the ceiling, and the only excitement of this lesson is waiting to see when it will fall down.

The noise level rises. I'm longing for the teacher to lose his temper and shout at the class to restore order. Communication has long become quite impossible. Neither teacher nor pupils can make themselves heard.

After the sixth lesson I ask a teacher, 'How on earth do you put up with this row?'

'What row? It was quiet today! You get used to it.'

The seventh lesson is a free period, for which I'm heartily thankful. I'm totally exhausted by the noise. How peaceful my day is in comparison! I can understand why John is so tired after mornings like this. I can't do anything about it, but at least now I know what he's talking about when he complains.

Suzanne's class has been doing long division in maths. Suzanne has been away with flu for three weeks and so we're going over it. She'd worked out one answer laboriously but didn't write it down immediately, so she's forgotten it.

She loses her temper and starts to cry. I tell her to work it out again. That was a wrong move! She explodes with rage, howls and bangs her fist on the table. What a good thing it is to be able to lose your temper and let off steam, I think to myself.

I wait for a little while. 'You're cross because you forgot the answer,' I venture.

'No, I'm cross with my maths book!' She screws up the exercise book.

'Do you want to burn it?'

'Yes, but I can't find the matches!'

'Here they are.'

'No!'

She crumples up the book again and throws it on the floor, followed by herself, screaming and kicking. Isobel daren't go near her; instead she comes and snuggles up to me like a kitten, as if to say, 'Look how good *I* am!'

Seeing me giving attention to Isobel annoys Susie even more. 'When you've finished being cross we can go and buy a new exercise book,' I suggest.

'I'm not going.'

'All right.'

So I take Michael into my room to practise a piece for his recorder lesson. Susie follows us. 'How much longer are you going to be with Michael?'

'We've nearly finished.'

Gradually she calms down. Everyone wants to go with us to buy the new exercise book. To make the journey worthwhile, we buy some ice cream and cough sweets at the same time. I spot the bread rolls and say, 'Actually I quite fancy a roll and a cup of coffee!'

'Oh yes, Mum, one each!'

We settle down in the kitchen. No one mentions maths again. But later on the whole thing is finished in ten minutes and neatly written out in the new book. The rest of Susie's homework doesn't take long either.

I have some mending and darning to do. Susie comes and sits by me. 'Phew,' I say, 'a tantrum like that is exhausting!'

'Why did *you* find it tiring? It was *me* that was shouting!'

But she's quite willing to help me. She tidies up the little ones' cupboard and makes the sandwiches for their tea.

And later, when I put the children to bed, Susie says in her prayers, 'Dear God, thank you for this lovely day!'

On the piece of paper Susie has just thrown on my desk, I read, 'You don't know how hard it is for me when nobody loves me except Teddy, Daddy and God! Why have we fallen out again? And why did you throw my present away? Susie.'

I am shocked at such sorrow in a nine-year-old. Of course I had been disappointed and cross, and had shouted at her. She'd been naughty. That's why I threw her painting in the waste-paper basket. But I didn't mean to hurt her so deeply.

I call out, 'Susie, come here!'

'No!'

'Come on! I'm sorry! Let's be friends again . . .'

She sits on my lap and sobs. We go and get the picture out of the bin together. It isn't torn, just crumpled. We iron it; the creases remain but we keep the picture. Susie is comforted. And since we're ironing, we go on ironing. Susie does the handkerchiefs and I do the shirts and blouses. I should have done them ages ago. No one interrupts us – the phone doesn't ring, no children rush in. I could almost enjoy ironing.

Then, out of the blue, Susie asks, 'Which would you rather have: the power to get everything you wanted by magic, or never to be sad again?'

'If I could get everything I wanted by magic, I could make sure I was never sad again!'

'No, you can't do that.'

She's right. Even a nine-year-old knows that there's no cure for sadness. What you need when you're sad is someone to iron shirts with.

I've been away for a day and a half. As I come in the front door, my case still in my hand, the children call out, 'Mum! Quick! Izzie's going to be sick!'

I run into the bathroom and hold her head.

'Aren't you even going to say Hello to me?' says Michael.

Suzanne, a little reproachful, adds, 'Mum, we were going to play the recorder some more – I've got a lesson in an hour!'

And Johnny says, 'Shut up, everyone! Don't forget I've got a Latin test tomorrow and I don't know my vocabulary yet!'

Theo is pleased to see me home again but has to go out straight away to get Isobel's medicine – she's got a middle ear infection and a chest infection. The door bell rings. Our neighbour from two doors down has come to complain because our dog . . . he can hardly say it . . . in his porch . . . and he trod in it . . . I really ought to . . .

'Yes, I'm coming!'

I get the feeling I'm home again.

All this might sound exaggerated. It sounds that way to me too. But that's how it happened! That's why I sometimes go away. But I like coming home too. It's nice to be needed – by husband and children, dogs and neighbours!

Sometimes I relax in front of the television. I find it so refreshing to have only one person at a time talking to me and not to have to answer.

That's how I happened to see the film about the Utomi Indians in Mexico. The Utomis go through various purification rites every year during their great festival. The faithful are sprinkled with twigs dipped in holy water, for nothing evil can touch someone who is 'clean'.

I found all this fascinating. Where else does such protection from evil exist? Such invulnerability, tranquillity – armed and shielded against the unexpected? I am so defenceless, so exposed to the things that wound and grieve me.

But ritual washing is not part of my tradition, not my language. Cultic purity is not an option for me. What is it that makes me strong and invulnerable in the face of insults, injustice, pain and sorrow? I'm not 'clean' and never will be. But in spite of that, God says to me, 'Come to me, you who are weary and burdened, and I will give you rest.'

He says this as he invites us to his table, where we kneel before him and he makes us clean; where we can stand up again and hear the words, 'Go in peace, the Lord is with you!' Not a ritual purity that makes us untouchable, but the presence of Jesus – his guidance and his strength, so that bad experiences don't just bounce off us; they turn into blessings.

> 'I am a stranger on earth;
> do not hide your commands from me.'
> *Psalm 119:19*

Because I am only a stranger on earth, with no rights, no resting-place, no security, because God himself has made me so small and weak, he has given me just one firm pledge of my destination: his Word. This one certainty he will never take away from me; he will keep his word to me, and through it he will let me feel his power. When I have his word with me, I can find my way in a strange land, justice in the midst of injustice, find security in the midst of uncertainty, strength for my work, patience in suffering.

Dietrich Bonhoeffer

4
Enjoy your children!

'Enjoy your children!' says Mrs Berger, who hasn't any children herself. 'They seem so happy and contented.'

'Yes, most of the time they are . . .'

Isobel smiles at the visitor. She doesn't want to miss the moment when Mrs Berger takes a bar of chocolate out of her handbag. But Mrs Berger does nothing of the sort. Instead she asks, 'Are you happy, Izzie?'

Isobel answers, 'Yes . . . what's happy, Mummy?'

'The way you feel now.'

'I feel . . . as if I'd like some bread and peanut butter.'

'Yes, that's it.'

To divert my attention from the typewriter to himself, Michael asks, 'Mum, why are you always writing stories and all that?'

'Because I enjoy it, and because I want to say that I like having you around and that you're not just a lot of work . . .'

'Us? A lot of work? I worked yesterday – don't you remember? I cleaned the whole house – I'm aching all over now!'

'Yes, you did a lot!'

'You'd never manage without us, would you?'

'Yes, that's right.'

'Mum, shall I switch the light on for you?'

'No, thanks.'

'I can go then, can't I, if you don't need me? Mum . . . Suzanne hasn't given the budgies any water!'

'She isn't even up yet.'

'Shall I wake her up?'

'No, she'll be cross.'

'Mum, I'm going now. What shall I put on? My best trousers?'

'No, you can put your jeans on.'

'My jeans? But you know they're too small. That's an idea – if I wear them I can draw on them, houses and everything. I could do it in school when I don't get my turn. Sometimes I never do get my turn. I'm too near the front, that's why the teacher doesn't see me. But I can see better at the front. If I turn round I can see everybody. Mum, my ear hurts! Do you think there's some dirt in it?'

'Yes, just a little.'

'Mum, how much longer is it going to take?'

'What?'

'Your writing.'

'I'm just going to stop.'

'Good, then you can help me get dressed.'

Michael and Cathy are flying a toy plane. It lands on the flat roof; so Michael climbs the tree against the wall of the house to get on to the roof. He loves climbing it in any case, although he's strictly forbidden to do it.

Cathy laughs at the sight of him scrambling up the tree. Those two are inseparable; they sit together in class and they always play together. Sometimes we tease them and say, 'You're just like an old married couple!'

Hearing Cathy laughing, Michael calls down, 'Cathy! We're a married couple, you're not supposed to laugh!'

'We're only engaged,' answers Cathy.

'Engaged? We're not!'

'Well, in love then.'

'Anything you say!'

After all this harmony, there are of course also days when they say they're never going to play together again – but that's usually forgotten after half an hour. Forgiving and forgetting is still easy at their age. Sharing is not so easy. Will they ever become sensitive to each other's needs? Will they become considerate and caring?

Isobel is watering the garden. The outside tap has been turned on again since yesterday, so the children can play with water as well as fire. She gives everything a good soaking, even the part of the garden which is already a swamp. The tap drips; and Tipsy, the dog, stretches his head to reach it.

'Come on, Tipsy!' says Isobel. She carefully turns the tap a little and gives him a drink from her cupped hand. And then some more; and then she wipes his snout – with her skirt.

'There, that's better, isn't it?'

Watching her, I think, 'She'll certainly be caring and know what love is.' And I pray, 'Lord, hold her in your hand and protect her. Surround her with love, so that she can always give love.'

I think of the verse from Psalm 27 which says, 'In the day of trouble he will shelter me; he will hide me under the cover of his tent.' In spite of all the trouble and care we take over our children, we can't really protect them inwardly or outwardly. We can't know what will one day be important to them. We can only pray for them; pray that their lives will not go by without their hearing the call of God and saying Yes to it, so that they will be safe in his protection. To know that God holds them in his hand helps us not just to cope with this life – but to live free from anxiety, to be completely happy.

Michael has to do an IQ test for his new school. We are doing our best to look cheerful and composed. Michael really *is* cheerful. He's been asked to identify colours and shapes and arrange them. He dismisses this as 'kids' stuff' but does it wrong. Then he has to repeat sentences and copy the word 'tree'. I intervene – it's not fair, I've never practised writing with him; after all we've got four children. 'Doesn't matter,' says the headmaster, 'we just want to see what he can do.'

Michael writes 'tree' as if he's being doing it all his life. I can't believe my eyes. The headmaster isn't satisfied with it. Of course, he doesn't say so; he talks about 'inadequate development of precise motor skills'.

Then Michael has to look at a picture of various fruits

with a train in the middle. 'Michael, what shouldn't be there?'

Without hesitation, Michael answers, 'The apple!'

'Why?'

'Because the train can't get through while the apple's in the way.'

'Michael, have another look – it's all fruit, there's just one thing that doesn't belong there.'

'The pear!'

'The pear?'

'Yes, I just said, 'cos the train can't get through.'

The headmaster gives up. Michael is not the least bit discouraged. He does reasonably well at fitting plastic pieces into the right spaces. I'm bracing myself for a negative decision. But when the headmaster finds out that Michael grew up with three languages in Papua New Guinea, he exclaims, 'Ah, that makes sense! Don't worry, we'll take him. You're ready for school, my lad!'

We go home. We've hardly been home a minute when the phone rings. It's the headmaster. 'Don't misunderstand me . . . I mean, it could be . . . well, after Michael went, I noticed a couple of plastic pieces were missing, and I need them for the next test. Can I ask whether perhaps he's put a couple of triangles in his pocket – by mistake, of course?'

'But we were all there watching!'

'Yes, but it could just be . . .'

'Michael . . . did you accidentally take those red and blue plastic shapes with you?'

'No – why should I want them? I put them under the bench because I couldn't fit them in.'

The headmaster takes a look. 'Yes, they're there. I do apologise . . .'

'Was that a test?' asks Michael.

'Yes.'

'Can I have something as a reward, then?'

'What would you like?'

'A hammock – then I could lie in it and make sure that the sparrows don't pinch the fluff out of the blackbirds' nests and take it to their cupboards. It isn't fair.'

Michael always wants to avoid anything that means extra effort. When his father's birthday is coming up, I suggest that we should read him a bit from the book 'Peter and the Apple' together.

'That would be a lovely surprise for him! Wouldn't you like to do it? He'd be so pleased.'

'Or I could give him a box of nails,' suggests Michael. 'Then he'll have something to work with.'

'Nails? For his birthday?'

'Yes, I can stick a candle in it if you want.'

We often wonder whether our children will find their way in life. Are they ready to work at things or do they expect everything to be given to them? Will they be open to other people, ready to work for peace in every situation?

When John was six, there was a time when he played at nothing but war. He swapped his harmless matchbox cars for tanks and bombers which he pushed around the floor with great enthusiasm. I couldn't stand it any longer, and tried to show him in words and pictures how terrible war is.

'I'd never *shoot* anybody!' he said. I was pleased. 'No', he went on, 'I'd put poison in their food instead.'

I think we must have read Snow White too often!

If our children have trouble controlling their tempers and keeping out of fights, they have no trouble at all with communication; we have too many visitors for that. Even at seven Suzanne would answer the door if we weren't in, and let the visitor in. She would ask if he wanted anything to drink, and her favourite question was, 'Have you got a cat as well?' Should the answer be negative, she would continue her conversation with the somewhat delicate question, 'Have you got a loose tooth too?' If the visitor had to deny this too, but showed sufficient interest in both subjects – cats and teeth – she would offer to show him her room; till at last we would arrive and rescue the victim from heaps of dolls and jigsaw puzzles – which Susie would regret greatly.

Isobel, too, enjoys being with people. The other day she sat under our neighbour's kitchen table setting the world to rights and above all repeating everything that we'd just been talking about at dinner. We always think of that possibility too late. But the neighbours are kind people, with children of their own, and they never tell us the whole of these conversations. Only occasionally they will ask, 'Tell me, is it true that you're going away tomorrow?' Imagination, wishful thinking and reality have been woven into a single fabric and passed on as solid fact.

Suzanne greets our neighbour, who's just popped in, with the words, 'Look! I sewed it myself!'

'All by yourself?'

'Yes, with Mummy. I sewed the straight bits and she did the rest.'

The dress has turned out well. Susie and I are both pleased with it. We've forgotten the tears, the laborious unpicking, the tantrums. She bought the material from her pocket money, and we sat together over paper patterns and at the sewing-machine. It all looks so easy, and they describe it so simply: 'Next put in the zip' – but it can end up in disaster, floods of tears and fury.

However, all that's behind us. What remains is the feeling that 'I know how to sew myself a dress – with a little help.' And later on she won't sit in front of a sewing pattern – as I sat today in front of a text-book – and give up before she's even begun.

'Sewing a dress and baking bread aren't hard!' she says. 'I don't know why some grown-ups can't manage it.'

She has her own sewing-machine, a box of remnants and old bits and pieces which she can make into conjurer's costumes or other things for dressing up. With these she can cut things up and spoil a bit here and there. We can let her do something wrong and still help her to make something out of it – something quite unforeseen.

In the same way we've discovered new recipes, such as the famous Susie's biscuits, a recipe we can't share because it's a secret.

All this takes time and trouble – for mother at least – but it means finding out by experience that it isn't such a disaster to make a mistake. We make so many and only live because God doesn't give each of us what we deserve but forgives us again and again.

Michael is having one of his 'No' days. On days like this I forget that tantrums are only tantrums, and I fall into bed at night exhausted. Only night doesn't come all that quickly. However, eventually it's six o'clock, and at Michael's request I read out a story about Mickey Mouse going to the moon.

'Why do you need space suits and helmets?' asks Michael.

'Because there's no oxygen on the moon,' I answer.

'No,' says Michael.

'Right, now get into the bath.'

'No.'

'Then I'll have to do my trick on my own!'

'What trick?'

'The one with the macaroni and shampoo.'

'Can I come too?'

'Yes.'

We make bubbles in the bath tub, mountains of bubbles which slowly roll over the edge of the tub. At last Michael's defiance evaporates in sheer delight. While I rinse his back and rub him dry with a warm towel, he hugs me with still dripping arms and says, 'Mummy, I do love you so much!'

'And I love you, too.'

I carry him to bed, a contented bundle.

Even Isobel, overwhelmed by the bubbles, forgets her usual jealousy. 'Can we do that every night?' she asks.

'No,' I reply.

Only Michael, Isobel and I are at home. So I ask them what they'd like to eat today.

'Rice Krispies and milk and stewed apples.'

'All right.'

While we're eating the steaming apples, Michael says, 'Mum . . . If I become a policeman, will you still recognize me?'

'Of course! We'll always recognize you!'

'Even with a uniform and a helmet?'

'Yes.' But why do you want to be a policeman?'

'What else can I be?'

I suggest about a dozen to him, including his usual favourite, a gardener. But then Isobel joins in, 'I want to be a policeman as well!'

'Oh good,' says Michael, 'then she can help me. Then I won't be afraid.'

With this satisfactorily settled, my two policemen finish their meal.

We're in the process of buying a terraced house. The plans are spread out in front of us on the table. We're discussing loft conversions and floor tiles, and I'm looking forward to the new fireplace we've decided on. Then Isobel says, 'You're just like the fisherman and his wife in my story book!'

'How's that?'

'You're always wanting a nicer house.'

Silence.

Isobel asks, 'Don't you like our house?'

'Yes, very much. But this house doesn't belong to us.

We only rent it, and we'd like a house of our own some day.'

My explanation is of no help either to Isobel or to myself. I'm deeply disturbed. Children are very quick to spot our tendency to want more all the time. It's not as if we're trying to buy a palace, only an ordinary terraced house. But we want something other than what we've already got. When children keep wanting to have things and are unwilling to give, we tell them off – but what about us?

We'll still buy the house, but we won't forget the story of the fisherman and his wife.

5
A thousand broken pieces?

I spend my time running around, organizing, tidying up, and never seem to come to an end of it all; and meanwhile I steal a glance at the important things outside: the interesting trips my husband goes on, the exciting conversations he has with colleagues and friends. He sees new things, has new experiences. His work has a tangible result; you can see the end-product, and success gives him the motivation to go on.

When I manage to get to my desk – when the anoraks have been hung up, the shoes sorted out, the wilting flowers watered – a long drawn-out wail comes from the garden, 'Mum, Torsten's thrown sand in my eye!'

I wash it out. Isobel goes back to the sand pit, I go back to my desk.

'Mum, can I take a book to the sandpit?'

Then Michael calls out, 'I'm just going out – when shall I come back?'

Before I can answer, the phone rings. A message for my husband. Then the doorbell starts. It's a friend of mine. 'I haven't seen you for so long – how's it going? What are you up to?'

'Oh, nothing much – come in!'

Of course, my husband gets interrupted as well. But he can get down to a specific project – a paper on something, or a seminar. Sometimes I'm jealous, and tell him, 'It's all right for you! You do all the big, important things – I only do the little odd jobs. You have exciting ideas and plans, and I spend my time writing shopping lists! You have consultations and discussions, read books and give lectures, and I spend my day saying a hundred times over, "Have you cleaned your teeth? Have you got your milk money? Where's your gym kit bag? Has the dog been fed? Have you done your recorder practice?" '

'Yes, you're right,' says Theo, 'but I have to do a lot of routine jobs as well. Every job has them; even if I do fly to the other end of the world. I still have to do all the odd jobs, even if I'm tired and haven't slept for two nights.'

'Yes, I know how tiring long flights are. And I know that there's routine work in every job, and things that seem useless or don't have any lasting result. But in my job there's *only* the boring little jobs. At least that's the way it looks sometimes.'

Of course there are other days when it all looks quite different. Then I see all those little things as if through a microscope, and even the smallest and most insignificant job becomes colourful, full of life and variety. My feelings are the microscope. When I feel like singing, when I'm thankful to God for the life he's given me, everything takes on a new colour. The children – without whom the day would often be quite difficult enough – become a wonderful gift from God. How much he gives me through them!

Isobel interrupts me for the fifth time. She sticks a ladybird, painted all by herself, on my hand and says, 'That's to give you good luck all the time!'

Michael wants to give me a treat as well, and empties his packet of Smarties on to my desk, 'Have the best one – the yellow one, it's just like the sun!' Sunshine and happiness.

My brother's right – I am lucky to have four children. I just don't always feel strong enough for all four at once! So Susie has to buy the book *A Surprise for Susie* herself – sometimes you have to treat yourself to something nice.

There's always so much to be done whether I feel like it or not: the curtain has to be hooked back on to the rail, that zip has to be replaced, the kitchen needs tidying up . . . But now and then I can also do something I enjoy – bake some bread, for instance. I love to see the lumpy, coarse mass gradually turn into a smooth, supple, heavy dough; I love to put the three long loaves, with the pattern I've scored on them, into the oven and smell the delicious fragrance making the whole house warm and cosy. The children can hardly wait until it's ready to eat.

Or planting the first pansies after the long winter . . . or cutting out a dress . . . all this enriches my life, so that every moment feels like my own. I can do something with my hands, create something, change something, try something new, and all this is part of the enjoyment of life.

'Thankfulness is a force before which all the powers of darkness surrender' says Herman Bezzel. And happiness – what is happiness? Being glad to do the thing that's nearest, not overlooking the ladybirds and the Smarties, and sinking into bed at night exhausted with the prayer, 'Lord, thank you for this day. Heal what I've spoiled. Forgive my discontentedness and my impatience. Help me to learn to live by your grace.'

A full life doesn't only mean achieving things, it means simply being alive. Being thankful and attentive to God, aware of his presence and open to receive all he has to give.

'True prayer is a kind of concentrated living: standing firm and silently waiting for the call which summons us not to achieve anything or do anything, but to become what we really are – presenting ourselves to God.'

Gerhard Ebeling

'In everyday life our soul seems to be a great big barn into which everything gets shoved indiscriminately from all sides, day by day, until it's filled to the roof with the ordinary. And so it seems to go on, our whole life long – till in the hour of our death all the odds and ends that made up our life suddenly get swept out of the barn all at once. But what will remain of us then, we whose whole life was made up of everyday hustle and bustle, fuss and bother? Will anything remain other than the few moments when the gift of love or real prayer crept shyly and timidly into a corner of that life full of everyday junk?

We can't pray consciously all the time, we can't escape from ordinary everyday life; we take it with us wherever we go, for we are made up of our everyday life – our ordinary hearts, our tarnished souls, our meagre love which makes even great things small and commonplace. And because of this the way can only lead through the centre of our everyday life, through its needs and its duties; because of this the ordinary cannot be conquered by escape, only by standing firm and letting ourselves be transformed. Therefore God can only be sought and found in the everyday world, and the everyday must become God's own day.'

Karl Rahner

Yuriko lived next door to us, with her family, for two years. When I think of her I always see her shredding white cabbage. For her it was something quite commonplace and ordinary. I could have watched her for hours. With what care and skill she worked! Quickly, but not in a hurry – enjoying what she was doing. Every movement was beautiful. She held the wedge of cabbage as if it were something quite precious. She was never sullen or indifferent, with her thoughts far away. She was totally intent on her task: she was cutting white cabbage, and nothing else.

So often I do two or three things at once. While I'm cooking, a cake is burning in the oven, the washing machine and dishwasher are running, and at the same time I'm doing something for the children. Nothing gets done properly, and I'm worn out.

But the way Yuriko cut vegetables was beautiful. Although she was working fast, tranquillity radiated from her. She liked doing it, she was glad that she could buy vegetables and cook them for her family, because her husband earned enough so that they didn't have to go hungry.

When the picture of Yuriko comes into my mind, then I know that that's how I'd like to do things: carefully, with dedication and concentration. To be completely involved in what I'm doing; to feel it totally. How refreshing that would be! I wouldn't get so exhausted; it's rushing about that spoils everything.

I couldn't do it all the time, but occasionally it must be possible to do just one thing at a time and be entirely intent on it – the way Yuriko used to cut vegetables.

Sometimes I dream about all the things I could do with the rubbish that gets thrown out in our street, if only I had a big shed, a little more time, a few tools, glue and dye and someone to help me.

'You know,' says my neighbour, who has five children, 'I've often thought that too! We'll make something new out of all the old broken things and then we'll rent a garage somewhere on the road out of town . . .'

Dreams like these give us the strength to see the children through all the drudgery and disappointments of their first few years at school, when they're learning to read and write, and to support them when they get to secondary school and have to start studying in earnest. In the meantime we have long telephone conversations about what we've found on the scrap heap – high-class porcelain, broken and half-finished things whose charms are increased in our eyes because we could make something out of them. We talk about our children and sometimes about ourselves: how to stand it when at 9.30 in the evening the children are still asking, 'I'd just like to know one thing; how do earthworms burrow into the ground?' . . . And as I'm exerting my last shreds of strength to find a convincing answer, Michael says, 'I know the answer! I just wanted to know if *you* knew.'

How can anyone get through this life without dreams? They don't have to be grandiose dreams, they just have to make time and space disappear. Dreams that will take me to a place where I don't have to tidy up or mend anything, go shopping or cook, and where I certainly don't have to waste my strength cleaning sticky kitchen cupboards. A place where I can do something I don't have to do. Something unnecessary, perhaps even pointless. Something nice and new. I'd like to print cloth again, with Melanesian and other patterns in red and orange or orange and yellow. And I wouldn't mind working with Marimekko, the Finnish lady, or just watching her working.

I dream of designing a range of cards: Christmas cards, for instance. Or cutting out pictures to go with words from the Psalms, words I identify with. I'd only need coloured paper, scissors and paste, music and a large table. Everything around me vanishes. I'm filled with happiness.

What makes me happy, makes my family less so. 'Aren't we going to eat *yet*?' asks John.

Even this question, a question of survival, only reaches me as if through a veil. Absent-mindedly I answer, 'Eat what you like, if you're hungry!' The children pounce on this calm offer of freedom, and I have peace and quiet for another half-hour.

Two cards have turned out well. I like them. There are scraps of paper everywhere. Who cares? I shall make some more cards, send them to a printer and have them printed. Before Christmas I'll be able to go into a shop and buy my own cards.

A pleasant dream. It looks as though it might even become reality. I feel really refreshed, as though I'd had a long holiday. The children have made the best they could of their mother's dreaming and left the kitchen in chaos; now they've gone out again. I clear the things and put them in the dishwasher, singing as I do so. It's good to be singing while I work again.

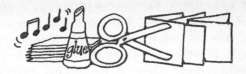

Some women startle their husbands with the statement, 'I haven't got a thing to wear', and open the wardrobe to prove it. My husband rarely hears that sentence; not because I'm so modest in my needs, but because I generally have such a clear idea of what I want in the way of dresses and blouses that I have to make them myself. Nevertheless, I do occasionally go out intending to buy rubber bands, cheese and margarine and come back with a new jacket and shoes!

No, the sentence that really worries my husband is, 'Hey, I've had an idea!' And since my best ideas arrive before I've got up in the morning (after that I'm too occupied with buttering bread, cutting open cartons of milk and hunting for schoolbooks), I often drag him out of his peaceful sleep with them.

Of course, I've learned to wait for an opportune moment to make these revelations. But no moment is ever really opportune. Not because Theo is too stubborn to accept anything new, but because he is always meeting new people and plans, new places and situations, and therefore likes to have a regular, peaceful routine at home.

I, on the other hand, satisfy my need for change by moving the furniture around. That might conjure up a picture of chaos, but it's not as bad as all that, since we don't have much furniture. What there is, is small, light and largely home-made – nothing old or valuable. When it comes down to it I'm happy just to move the table out of its corner and replace it with a comfortable arrangement of cushions to create a space for listening to music, reading or watching TV. The children and the dog snuggle up to me immediately.

But I must admit that my 'ideas' are not confined to furniture. They also encompass people – visitors we ought to invite, new hobbies, things we neither need nor, mostly, want to do. I do these things when my husband is away on long business trips, when I'm missing his reliability and sense of order – when I'm missing him, in fact. When we write long letters to each other and think of each other much more than we do when we're together. When we let our worries about each other turn into prayers for each other.

Our neighbour in Papua New Guinea used to fetch Suzanne in the car, when she collected her own children from primary school. On the way home Suzanne would recount everything she'd learned: she'd finished her second reading book, done three columns of sums, written a whole side . . . and Rua would let out a whistle of admiration now and then. Once she was a little slow in responding. So Susie went on with her account. When the whistle still didn't come, Susie whistled herself. Everyone deserves appreciation! It's not just for children, however – I need it too.

When the family is shovelling in the food I've put before them – food that means planning and shopping, carrying home, preparation, cooking, laying the table, serving, clearing up, washing up, putting away – I sometimes give up waiting and say, 'Nice meal, ha?'

'Mm.'

'It's good of you to say so!'

Everyone laughs. Johnny says, 'It really is nice, Mum, so nice that we haven't any time to say so.' I'm more or less placated.

I remember the last afternoon of our holiday in Denmark, when I thanked Theo for the things I'd particularly enjoyed. The children did the same. And then Theo asked, 'And what are you going to thank Mummy for?'

Silence.

'For bringing us into the world?' said Susie hesitantly.

'Is that all?' asked Theo.

'No! The other day when I bought an ice cream she gave me some extra money!'

John remembered, 'And me!'

As often happens, Isobel appeared to save the situation. She edged closer to me and said, 'Mum, it's nice at our house!'

I thought to myself happily, 'That makes all the trouble worth it!' Then, unmoved, she continued, 'But it's even nicer at Sarah's. They have apple juice there!'

You can't expect recognition, public or private, every day. They say that the low value put on housework makes housewives ill. One housewife in eight is on the brink of total breakdown, the statement from the organization for the welfare of mothers says. That's why women should defend themselves against daily discrimination, and make their needs and wishes felt. They should start to search actively for their true selves; they need to increase their sense of self-worth . . .

I ought to be pleased at this prospect of an improvement in my situation, but it all sounds like a rather joyless duty to me. I'd like to see the options of the housewife and mother in a rather more positive light. What a luxury to be able to plan your own time! What freedom to be able to do something without being paid for it! 'He who loses his life will save it,' says Jesus.

'It's always the women who pour out the coffee!' a colleague once said at a theological conference. 'I get annoyed by it!' Yes, I see her point, but on the other hand I don't mind doing it. It isn't degrading. I could say something friendly to someone as I pour out their coffee. Or I could hold out my cup and say, 'I do so enjoy my coffee when you pour it out.'

How seriously I take the subject of 'the right to recognition and personal growth' depends on whether there is someone who loves me, and on whether I believe in a God who wants me to be happy and enjoy life. If you can hear God saying, 'You are valuable in my sight' then you can live and give your life for others – perhaps for someone special who says, 'Look here, I can't be alone any more. I just can't.'

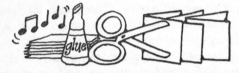

Am I really enjoying my life? You might think the life of a housewife and mother is one of the happiest there is. Humming quietly, she glides over the hygienically gleaming floors of her house, looks at her reflection in the spotless tiles of her kitchen, admires her carefully arranged hair and her satin-smooth hands. With a clear conscience, she piles up the soft, clean washing. Dirty windows – if there can be such a thing – are transformed by a mere touch into brightly-shining panes. Contented and well rested, she serves her work-weary husband an instant meal and offers her children essential vitamins in the form of bread and margarine which they accept gratefully. If, by some inconceivable chance, she should be tired, a tonic will settle that. To complain would be ungrateful. Her husband gives her a kiss – a sure sign of happiness. Her husband – in his clean shirt full of sunshine and the smell of spring . . .

It's been raining here for five weeks. Maybe that's why

I can't believe the adverts. We don't have a machine that can carry shopping or empty dustbins, or a computer that knows how to sort socks into pairs and put them in drawers. There's no button with which one can switch off the noise of children quarrelling and shouting at each other, of dogs who bark every time the phone rings, of budgies and other friends of the family.

That's why I collapse into bed exhausted at the end of the day. In spite of soft washing and all those vitamins my conscience isn't clear. 'Another day over!' I think to myself. 'I was impatient with the children and unfair to them. The meal was made in a hurry, without any affection . . . tomorrow I'll do it differently.'

Is this life? Am I enjoying it? Sometimes I'm too tired to be thankful or joyful.

But life is happening now; not later, when the children are grown up and I'll be glad if they ring up now and then. It's now that I have to try to squeeze out a few moments in the hectic day to switch off and recover. It's no good to search for 'reality' amid all this 'unreality'. This varied everyday life is my reality now. And the point is, says Bonhoeffer, to find God in the things he gives us.

What we need is to accept that the present is the place where we must live and work and experience God's grace. We would like to do something grand and lasting. But Luther once said, 'To make a sad, despondent man happy is greater than to conquer a kingdom.'

'Small things really are small. But to be faithful in small things is a big thing.'

Augustine

If I only had one day to live, I know what I'd do. I'd celebrate all day, with Theo and the children, with our friends. I'd give away all my things, have a communion service, sing songs and listen to music.

And every so often I'd cry, for I do love it so, this life – colourful and difficult, comical and draining, full of surprises and opportunities, with all its experiences of joy and blessing.

But maybe I'd be completely dazed and full of anxiety. Anxiety for my family, and anxiety because I don't know what it will be like to die. I hope then I'd still be able to pray,

> 'When I tread the verge of Jordan
> Bid my anxious fears subside;
> Death of death, and hell's destruction,
> Land me safe on Canaan's side;
> Songs of praises, songs of praises
> I will ever give to thee.'

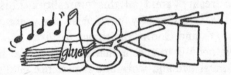

'That's sheer extravagance,' people say. The Bible records how a woman breaks an alabaster jar full of real, expensive perfume and anoints Jesus' head. How many more important things could have been done with the proceeds! Feeding the hungry, for example . . .

Money can be wasted. But time? Time is life. When we love, we are extravagant; for the only thing we want is to show how much we love. We pour out our love and our lives, and receive it all back many times over. He who gives, receives – receives real life.

Only when we give praise to the God who made us and

sent his Son to rescue us do we really live. Worship is a part of our lives which is in danger of being lost. How far we are from the speaker of Psalm 17, who says, 'When I awake, I shall be satisfied with your likeness'! Spending time resting in God's presence, being strengthened and refreshed – how much that could do for our restlessness, discontent, hurry, frustration, anxiety, spiritual hunger! 'He will give you the desires of your heart' says Psalm 37. Once I went to a communion service where they gave out cards with prayers and meditations before the service. I read the sentence, 'You are there and you look lovingly at me – thank you!'

Nothing had moved me for a long time as much as that sentence did. Jesus looks lovingly at me – that's how I stay alive. I get enough critical looks, questioning looks, sceptical and non-committal looks. But I need someone to look at me lovingly. A love that smooths the frown from my face and reaches through to my heart. A look that moves me so deeply that I repeat this sentence again and again until I'm completely immersed in its reality, in the presence of Jesus. His love heals me and at the same time shames me; how much love God lavishes on me! Why this waste? So that I will give away a drop of this overflowing love and pass on to others the extravagant love of God.

Just one word would be enough; one word from God that gets through to me. But his word – the Bible – is often so strange and remote.

'The little prince,' wrote Saint-Exupéry, 'went away, to look again at the roses. "You are not at all like my rose," he said. "As yet you are nothing. No one has tamed you, and you have tamed no one. You are like my fox when I first knew him. He was only a fox like a hundred thousand other foxes. But I have made him my friend, and now he is unique in the whole world." And the roses were very much embarrassed. "You are beautiful, but you are empty," he went on. "One could not die for you." '

The little prince had tamed the fox and the fox had told him his secret, 'It is only with the heart that one sees rightly.' If only we could approach the word of God in the same way. If only we could make friends with it. Not to be 'chummy' with God, in a false kind of way; but to get so close to him that his word becomes unique amidst the flood of words around us. A word that lets us catch a glimpse of God's secrets and the miracles he does among us, speaking to us and transforming us. So that, in the words of Bonhoeffer, 'God's Word comes to us as a force in our lives which leaves no moment untouched.'

One word would be enough. Perhaps one line which stays with us through the day as a counter-balance to all the many and varied impressions which assault us. We cannot earn the right to have nothing but pleasant experiences, to have God talking to us all the time. But we are ready, we are waiting and praying. God speaks through a word which I hear or which suddenly occurs to me; through something someone says or writes, something I read or reply to. A word which I carry with me until it becomes a prayer. When that happens, heaven and earth meet.

It still seems a miracle to me, that in a moment of inner and outer isolation, the words from Isaiah 42 came into my mind, 'A bruised reed he will not break, and a smouldering wick he will not snuff out.' It was a verse I had known a long time, but this time I heard it as if God himself were saying it to me, to keep me alive.

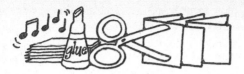

Each moment belongs to me. The moment when I'm waiting for my husband or the children. The moment when I'm sitting and listening to someone else talking. The impatient moments and the sad moments. Sadness caused by words unspoken or by angry words, by chances of happiness I missed or life that wasn't lived to the full. Moments, days and periods of my life without God.

'How we've thrown away our life,' says Mother Teresa, 'if it's full of ourselves instead of God!'

Each and every moment belongs to me. I feel that most when I'm happy. When I'm pleased with the children and thank God for this life. Thankful that I am loved and can love in return.

But the moments full of anxiety are part of my life as well. And those full of peace because God has taken away my fears. And the happiness of giving to others what God has given me, sharing my life with others.

All these moments, bright or dull, cheerful or despondent, quiet or hectic – they all belong to me. But I can't fit them all together. When I examine and judge, weigh up and condemn, they fall apart into a thousand pieces. But when God sees my life and yet still looks at me lovingly, it all comes together. Then I can say, 'All my moments, Lord, are fleeting and imperfect – but yours is the kingdom, the power and the glory, for ever and ever, Amen!'